Healing The

Wounds

Of A Fatherless

Generation
Devotional

Varn Brown

Dedication

I dedicate this book to my dad, Rev. La'Vern Brown. I preached at several of his church anniversaries before he passed. I am my father's son. I see a lot of myself in him. I'm glad to take up where he left off. The Spirit of Lord said, "The previous generation has slain its thousands. Now, David his tens of thousands." I'm doing my best to make it so.

Contents

Introduction

Welcome to the *Healing The Wounds Of A Fatherless Generation Devotional* book. With joy, I present these snippets of father blessings, encouragement and yes, sometimes corrections to you.

A few years ago, after the first book, I started the "Healing The Father Wound" blog on Facebook. I wrote blogs for about two years; a couple of times a week and it's still going. It's funny to me; I would have some of my friends, brothers and sisters say to me, "Varn, why are you writing about the past? Why discuss something so painful?

I would say to them, "It's ministry for me especially for others that are still stuck in the past and their pain. Then I would say, if I have to go there to confront some of the pain to help a few, I will. I blogged about pushing past the pain, journey to healing through forgiveness, how to get unstuck and progress into wholeness.

I charged other men to be the solution, with the need still so great for spiritual fathers not just physical fathers. I have already seen some of the harvest of those precious seeds. I know that it will multiply even so much more in the future.

Hence, the HTWOFG Devotional was birthed from all the blogging. The Holy Spirit and my wife Earma said to me, "Varn, all this needs to be in a book." It's a compilation of a lot of those inspired blogs to help fathers and their kids heal.

We had to select fifty-two favorites. The book was getting too big with over 100 devotionals. So, here we go. Every word, which you read will have been a word of the over flow from me about the fatherless and father wound issues.

After I wrote the first book, it took about two years for me to let it all come out for me and the people I influence. With help from the Holy Spirit and me in tow, he let me know when it was time to come to an end. The Lord gave me a word. Some of you may remember I titled it, "I've come to a conclusion."

And I did, I believe that the Lord will do the same for you. So, be on the lookout for the conclusion. He will allow you to come to a good conclusion in him. So get ready, the journey continues.

With that said, life is a beautiful thing; all you have to do is have an ear to hear and eyes to see. This is why we should do our best to keep a clean life before the Lord. Because, if our life is clogged with worldly distractions, addictions and ungodly self-ambition, we tend to miss what's standing, and being said, right before our very eyes.

Today, I was thinking about the plight that's before fathers, sons and daughters of broken families. I was talking to a friend of mine, who is a single parent. He was telling me of his problems with his daughter wanting to go and see her mother. He told me all the reasons why she shouldn't go.

I looked at him and said, "No matter how many problems or reasons that may come up, it still would be better for her to go and see her mother." Even though, it may be very painful. Now, you know I'm not talking about an abusive situation.

Just the pain of a mother or father not being there for a child, makes the child mad. And it's so very easy for a mom or dad to just say, "Well, that's ok, you don't have to go this time," because they're already mad at each other.

That would be the wrong thing to do. Now, I know this from life. My life as a son of divorced parents. And, as a father, that went through a divorce with sons. My advice to my friend was, let her go and see her mother, even if she don't want to go.

When she is older, she will thank you for encouraging her. Even though, it may be a little awkward, don't try to rescue her. In this opportunity, there's a chance that the relationship will grow stronger and stronger.

Do you know that you were known even before you were in your mother's womb and gifted by God? If you think about it, us as humans never apologize for giving a gift. So why should God? In Romans 11:29, the writer explained, "For God's gifts and his call are irrevocable." Meaning, God has no apology and certainly does not take them back.

With that said, I was thinking the other day and being grateful about some of the last things that I remember my father did for me before he left this earth. One of them was he ordained me as a Baptist minister. Another one is the fact that he walked before me what it means to fall and get back up.

After he ordained me in the ministry, the Lord graced me to preach at several of his church anniversaries before his passing. I am my father's son, I see a lot of myself in him and I'm glad to be taking up where he left off. Saul has slain his thousands, David his tens of thousands.

As you read this devotional, you must ask yourself the question I and many others have had to ask, are we hindering God? As a son, we must learn to forgive. If you don't forgive, it's like plaque in a vein, it will clog the blood flow and can eventually stop the heart. We must forgive; it is as natural as the blood that flows throughout our body that gives us life itself. Besides all that, God commands us to forgive.

If I hadn't forgiven my father, for his mistakes I would have passed down unbelievable pain and trouble to the next generation. Now, I know everything isn't perfect, but no one is a second generation alcoholic or beating each other.

You see, we must jump leaps and bounds to see Christ come forth in our families. So, make sure you are doing the least of things and forgive. Because if you are not, you aren't receiving God's best for yourself or your family.

Father God has given me a platform that crosses many denominations and non-denominational churches among the people of God. In other words, many different kinds of Christian believers read my work. So, before it comes up, I thought I would clear the air a bit.

These commandments that I give to you today are to be on your hearts. Impress them on your children. Talk about them when you sit at home and when you walk along the road, when you lie down and when you get up. Tie them as symbols on your hands and bind them on your forehead. Write them on the doorframe of your houses and on your gates. —Deuteronomy 6:6-9

As a son, I was raised with the word of God set before me. As a father, we raised our sons with the word of God ever before them. Our sons, as loving fathers, are raising their children with the word set before them. If you want to have a successful family life, you will set the word of God ever before your family and children. You will have good success!

Varn Brown

Day 1: Father God and What He Did for Me

Back in 1983, the grace of God came to me and I got born again. My cup of abomination was full; it had run its course in my life. The Lord decided that it was time for my life to be harvested for the kingdom of God. So, the hedges were removed. The enemy was used to drive me into the arms of Jesus.

Sin had caught up with me. So, I had no choice but to surrender. I came out with my hands raised up to the Lord and said, 'Lord, I surrender.' I'm still saying it to this day. To be very real, the enemy was trying to take my mind. According to him, I was headed to the Psych ward. But I gave my mind, my heart, my whole self to the Lord instead. He, graciously, accepted it and restored me.

This is where it all began, this is what this devotional is all about, the title, *Father God and What He Did For Me*. I must say, the only reason I was able to change my life was because of the baptism of the Holy Spirit. I am, so thankful, for the grace of God and his precious gift.

My first order of change was I stopped going out to clubs. The Spirit of Lord removed the blinders from my eyes. I could clearly see what the whole club scene was all about. Satan and his imps doing their earthly schemes that he has done for eons and eons to enslave humanity and drag them to a Devil's Hell.

So. once I saw clearly, I was out the doors to never return. Then the Lord set it up for me to receive him as my Lord and Savior. Every morning, I would leave my job from Denny's as a cook, after working a grave shift.

I would get home, cut on the T.V and Jimmy Swaggart would be preaching the gospel like he would do every morning. With that long finger pointing at me out of the television, he would say, "You need to be saved!"

I ran from making that decision for a good while but one particular morning it would change me for the rest of my life. From that time, my life has not been the same. After that powerful change, the Lord set me up for the next one.

Now, I know I'm gonna get in a few people's stuff right here. But, sometimes, it's needful for some to come to the power of the truth. Because it is that 'same power' that raised Jesus from the dead. Yes, the same 'resurrection power' is what I'm talking about. The next step for me was, I received the baptism of the Holy Spirit.

Receiving Jesus in my heart after a month of deciding to make the decision, I did. I was staying with my sister Charlotte and told her of my decision. The Lord used her to direct me to the level that God had for my life. She introduced me to this radical Caucasian guy named Scotty. He was a wild man for Jesus! When we met, he invited me to his mother's house. He sat me down at their dinner table and explained the gospel and its power more correctly.

Scotty took me to every scripture in the New Testament about receiving the baptism of the Holy Spirit. After about an hour or so, in the word of God, he prayed with me and asked the Lord to fill me with his Spirit. God did just that.

I was filled with the Holy Spirit. I started crying, laughing and speaking in tongues all at the same time. To this day, my life has never been the same. A power from God has come; a power has come to serve the Lord. Then we got up right away and went into the streets. We shared the gospel with people and won some to the Lord.

My point for writing this is to let you know, if you want to make a change for the Lord, you will need his power. We, as humans, can't do it in our own flesh. In our human strength, if we could, Jesus would not have had to die for us, humanity. So, when I say to you that the word of God says, "Come out from among them and be ye separate." You can't say to me, "Varn I can't." Why? Because Jesus has made a way for us through the Cross.

There is a power and that power flows through Emanuel's veins; the same power that raised Jesus from the grave dwells in you, if you have received him. So, my prayer is that you make the change. If not already, invite Jesus into your heart as Lord and Savior. Then ask Father God to fill you with his Holy Spirit. He will do it for you just like he did for me. Finally, allow Father God to become your father! Keep going with me, next time I describe the new season that's headed your way...

Touch no unclean thing and I will receive you. I will be a father to you and you will be my sons and daughters, says the Lord Almighty. —II Corinthians 6:17

Day 2: A New Season

I was a young adult when it was time for me to make it on my own after high school and college. Most of us don't, I never really thought about it, as it was happening. I just figured that it was time for me to make it on my own.

When you are young, you don't think about who you are leaving, because you are so excited about what will be before you in the future. But, what was most important to me began to change.

He's Gone

I was away from home, about a year or so. I was in a club when my brother came up to me and said, "Grandpa is gone." I must say; I really didn't get it at first but it would sink in later that night.

My grandfather had been a *father* for me the last ten years of my life. It never crossed my mind that he, the mighty force, would one day pass away. Now, Grandma always said the Lord would soon one day come and take her home to glory. We would, lovingly say, "Grandma, you ain't going nowhere," and smile at her.

But to say the least, when my Grandpa died, my whole life shifted. He was, almost, like god to me. I thought he would never leave me. I guess that's why the Lord didn't let me be there when he transitioned. He had mercy on me; so that I could bear it.

Grandpa always sat on his front porch. After, a long day of work, he was on that porch, barefooted, with his Bible, singing or twiddling with his knife and a piece of wood. I would see him there. As I was leaving him, for the last time; I wouldn't know it, he was faithful at his watch over me.

By this time, it had been many years ago for me. I was reminded of this story in this season of transition in my life, right now. In this case, my grandfather is not there watching from the front porch. No, he's long time gone. But our Lord has sent me spiritual fathers, and one in particular to watch over me. I am very thankful.

A New Season Has Come

Just like when it was time for me to start on a new journey and take a leap by faith, it has come me again. Likewise, in the times before, I'm excited. My spiritual father is on the porch. I'm a bit sad to leave.

But in this case, I have a greater mission. I am being sent to see the kingdom of God more established in the earth. I am not afraid this time, for God is with me. He is my sword, my shield and my buckler.

Even though, I am reminded of the season when I left home for the first time and it brings me a little sadness. This time, I am emboldened, because I know my heavenly Father is with me.

My spiritual father has got my back and is in agreement with me. As I left, he was faithful and like always sitting in that same spot on the front porch cheering me on. Love you Papa! Thanks for being so patient with me over the last twenty years.

Day 3: Healing The Father Wound

As he went along, he saw a man blind from birth. His disciples asked him, "Rabbi, who sinned, this man or his parents, that he was born blind?"

"Neither this man nor his parents sinned," said Jesus, "but this happened so that the work of God might be displayed in his life. As long as it is day, we must do the work of him who sent me. Night is coming, when no one can work. While I am in the world, I am the light of the world." John 9:1-5

Over years the Lord has always positioned my wife and I to do different things in the Kingdom of God. Sometimes, it turned out be extraordinary things like help start an Armorbearer team in our local church when no one knew what it was. He led us to feed the poor and homeless. He led us to start altar ministry in time it was not the most popular thing to do.

Surprisingly, those assignments did not come with a lack of its own controversy. I said that to make a point about this group that I blog about to help the fatherless. One of the things said the most about the blog is 'you shouldn't bring up the past or you may get sucked in it again.'

Christ has redeemed us from the past. There is truth to both statements. We must understand whether we talk about it or not Christ has made the sacrifice for us to be free.

This is how I see it, in John 9, the disciples saw the blind man and they say to their Master Jesus, "Lord who caused this sickness the man himself or his father." The disciples want to know what caused the blindness. Jesus said to them no, the causes weren't him nor his parents.

This scenario is the same as in the case when they told Jesus, his friend Lazarus, had died. Yet he waited before going to see about Lazurus and his two sisters, Mary and Martha. They asked him why he waited. The answer was, 'so that God would get the glory.' In the case of the blind man and his parents, the answer was the same. Jesus said the reason the man was blind was so that God would get the glory.

So, for any one that would question me about why I speak or blog about a father wound and believe that God can heal it. The answer would be, so that God will get the glory.

Jesus did say there are time restraints that are on these situations. He said that it is day time now and we can only work while it is day. But night cometh when no one can work. So, as long as the Holy Spirit is here we can do the work of the lord but once He is gone we can work no longer.

When I speak of a the healing of a father wound, I know that its much bigger than me. I'm only a man. I know that I don't have all the answers. But, I do have an experience that the Lord brought me through and the Holy Spirit. When speaking of a person being delivered of the hurt of past abuse, I have to trust the Lord to do his job in that manner, that's where He rules.

You don't have to worry; I won't be having a class where we all sit in a circle and tell of all our pains and abuses. I'm pretty sure it helps because confession is good for the soul. But I know that is not my path right now this is only a devotional! Even so, with that said, I know the power of words and the power of God mixed with our faith! Who knows what will happen. For now, here are a few things that helped me and a lot of other people:

1. **Confession and acknowledgement:** It is good for the soul. If you have been sinned against or you have caused the sin. It has to be confessed in the right atmosphere speaking of any father hang-ups and issues.

2. **Forgiveness:** Forgiveness is always a must, to not forgive could block God's hand in healing you. We must give forgiveness and receive it.

3. Journey: It is a walk of faith, once you have confessed and acknowledged it. We must walk our confession out with faith believing and trusting God to do a complete work of faith in us.

This is process and we should trust the Lord that he will finish. I, personally, believe that as we are faithful in church and obedient to God, a complete deliverance will come. Sometimes, these days, some people don't stay faithful long enough to be completely healed. Make sure that's not you. Stick with God and watch what he will do for you.

Day 4: Speaking Of A Father Wound

Some people would say, well speaking of a father wound is like bringing up a past hurt that you don't want to speak about, ever. I can agree that it may be painful, but it's better than going around wounded and being hateful and not knowing why. Being mad at every male figure you come in contact with. That would be one of the signatures.

I'm only saying, if you have a wound you can ask the Lord to heal it and be on your happy way. But the thing is, you may need more than a prayer, it may take a process. Like talking about it, forgiving, confessing, crying, seeking God about it.

Just because it happened in the past doesn't mean it's dealt with, acknowledging it may be all you need to do. Just because it was very painful doesn't excuse you from dealing with it. God is faithful.

I remember my last conversation with my father. For several years before my dad left this earth and went to heaven, my wife and I would travel to Arkansas from Texas and preach for my father's church anniversary.

The Lord graced me to do it about three times but the last time we had a small misunderstanding. You see, the last time I preached for him, I felt led to say while giving my message, "Where are the men?" I said the church should be full of men. I said that because in that season, the Spirit of the Lord was beginning to send men back to the church. So, most churches were beginning to, if not full with men.

It was in the midst of the season when Promise Keepers was at its peak and Bishop Jakes started Man Power where there were thousands of men gathering in the name of Christ. I think my Dad got a little miffed at me. So, I went back to Dallas.

Whenever Earma and I would go, we would have to sacrifice because we were Armorbearing and helping start our new team of armorbearers at Covenant Church.

Also, we were still preaching in the jails every weekend. So, we had to in the old terms, "Go out of the way" to go preach in Arkansas. This last time, I would see him; he and my uncle Napoleon Gillespie were standing together talking. I had just got there and about to say hello to both, he and my dad.

If you know me, you know I started talking and boasting of the Lord and said to my Uncle Nate, I would like to come and preach at his church. Before he could say anything, my Dad said something like, "He's not faithful; he won't come." I had forgotten that fourth year, my dad invited me. I didn't make it because we were still a little mad at each other because of that statement about the men.

My dad could be pretty tough. I would let him win all the battles in conversation. I forgave him. I know he had a hard shell but his heart meant well.

I wish I would have pushed a little harder to go. But I stayed here in Dallas and served in my Church. That was the last time I saw him, but I have no regrets.

The Lord doesn't surprise me with the things he does. At my father's funeral, the Lord gave me a word to say. At that moment, I didn't know how profound it would be. I said, "My father did the best with what he was given, now what will you do with what you've been given?

I'm still learning from that statement to this day! I know I will see him in Heaven. Love you, Dad!

Day 5: My Father's Story

I've noticed a few things over the years of ministry in the area of father wounds. First of all, I've noticed that a root of the wound stays there because of un-forgiveness. In our human bodies, God put a natural propensity to heal itself. Hence, we have scabs and the drying and healing of wounds.

The same happens in our inner man. But when that natural healing is blocked, hindered, re-opened, the wound festers, right? So it is with the father wound. The wound stays in place because of the trespass that was made against them. Yes, it was very wrong. But the problem about this is, the recipient (the trespassed against one) stays stuck there, up a creek without a paddle, so to speak.

At my father's funeral, there was a little situation that I noticed that could've caused a problem but thank the Lord it didn't. You see, the church was split right down the middle, it seemed to me. Maybe me and a few others were the only ones to notice. Looking from the pulpit, out through the congregation, I saw to the left my mother's side of the family.

My brothers and sister all had blank stares on their faces. I knew why; it was from all the pain, drunkenness and un-forgiveness that my father brought to the family over the years. On the right side of the church, was my father's side including his last wife along with his spiritual sons; everyone on that side was wailing because of his death.

I have to admit I shed a few tears for my father's passing. I did love him as my whole family did despite the trouble that his life caused. I was sad that he passed prematurely; he was only sixty-five.

As I have already discussed, in later years, the Lord graced me with a relationship with him enough that I preached several of his church anniversaries. He ordained me as a Baptist minister. I was very thankful for that and the time spent with him.

The reason why I'm sharing all this with you is because I want you to know that I was able to forgive my father. I forgave him for almost killing my mother and breaking up our family. Because of him being a drunkard for a time in his life, we all suffered.

But this is what helped me; I found out that he, my father, had a story too. To make a long story short, the first time my father met his father he was twenty-four years old. When his father saw him, he came into the house where my father was sitting, walked through and said, "Hey Lavern." He kept walking. That was his greeting that he received from him meeting his dad for the first time. That is what he was given in his life as a son.

So, before the funeral I asked the Lord what should I say of my father as an encouraging word for me and the family. This is what came to me. I told his short story that I just shared with you and then I challenged the congregation with, "My father did the best with what was given to him. Now what will you do with what you have been given?"

A few months ago, one of my brothers said to me, "Varn, why do you want to bring up the past and speak of it. We should leave it all behind." My answer to him was, "If I have to speak of my past to save a few from much pain, I will."

Many of you know my testimony about my father wound, my healing and the spiritual fathers God sent to me. If not already, get a copy of my original book, *Healing The Wounds Of A Fatherless Generation*. My father story, Pushing Past the Pain To Forgiveness, Grandpa Ford was a God-man and much more.

Day 6: A Message From Father God

Jesus is coming and he shall appear in the clouds, with a blast of a trumpet we that are ready for his appearing will be caught up with him in the sky to go to the prepared place, where we will be with him forever. There will be on earth, a tribulation, that will last seven years and the devil will persecute the people that are left behind.

The persecution and trouble will be so bad, even death will flee from them. An angel will be sent to chain that old serpent the Devil, who will be bound for a thousand years. Then there will be a reign that will last a thousand years with Jesus the Christ and us Saints that were caught up with him will be there.

At the end of a thousand-year reign Satan, that old serpent, will be let out and will deceive the nations. Christ will come and destroy him with his holy fire and we will see him no more. Then there will be the "Great White Throne Judgment" where all humanity great and small will be judged and their works weighed before a mighty God. Read the Bible Book Revelation.

Humanity will be judged for not receiving Jesus Christ. And the body of Christ will be judged or weighed for what they did, or didn't do with Christ. And the rewards that He gives will be an eternal reward and will last forever throughout eternity.

Where will you be standing? Which side of the judgment seat will you be on, the right or the left? There may be still time, choose before it's too late! Or will you be able to stand confident with the faithful ones in Christ and say, "I've done my best in Christ and I'm not ashamed."

We must not forget that Christ Jesus is our blue print. He came and lived a righteous life for us as an example, so we could do the same. Proving that the life he lived, we could do the same through the power of the Holy Spirit.

Through his beautiful work, we won't have an excuse like it's too hard or I was afraid. There will be no place to run and or hide. Romans 2:5

Don't let stubbornness or an unrepentant heart cause you to store up wrath against yourself for the day of God's wrath when his righteous judgment will be revealed. God will give to each person according to what he has done.

To those who by persistence in doing good seek glory, honor and immortality, he will give eternal life. But for those who are self-seeking and who reject the truth and follow evil, there will be wrath and anger.

There will be trouble and distress for every human being who does evil, first for the Jew, then for the gentile, but glory honor and peace for everyone who does good. For God does not show favoritism.

I am doing like our brother did in the wilderness, John the Baptist, I'm proclaiming with my voice saying, "The dreadful day of the Lord," is coming and we must prepare for it by faithfully doing the righteous acts of Christ. We must position ourselves through obedience to the word of God before it's too late!

Let us hold unswervingly to the hope we profess, for he who promised is faithful. And let us consider how we may spur one another on toward love and good deeds. Let us not give up meeting together, as some are in the habit of doing, but let us encourage one another and all the more as you see the day approaching.

If we deliberately keep on sinning after we have received the knowledge of the truth, no sacrifice for sin is left, but only a fearful expectation of judgment and raging fire that will consume the enemies of God. Anyone who rejects the Law of Moses died without mercy on the testimony of two or three witnesses.

How much more severely do you think a man deserves to be punished who has trampled the son of God under foot, who has treated as an unholy thing the blood of the Covenant that sanctified him, and who has insulted the Spirit of grace? For we know him who said, "It is mine to avenge; I will repay", and again, "The Lord will judge his people". It is a dreadful thing to fall into the hands of the living God. — Hebrews 10:23-31 Are you ready?

Day 7: Do What The Father Does

Are you fathered or just doing your own thing? The reason I ask this question is all through the New Testament, Jesus made this statement and He would say. "I can only do what I see my Father do."

And there is no greater example that we should live by. You know, the Anointing only flows from the head down. God Himself has set up this chain of authority structure and the direction that it flows. Now the question is, and you know it's coming.

Do you have a father or a spiritual father, from which the anointing flows? Speaking of the anointing, you know the oil is always poured on the head first, then the hands and throughout the body to the feet. We, as the body of Christ, must always flow in the correct flow of authority that our Lord has set up in his church.

To not flow within this line of structured authority would leave you uncovered, unprotected. A body without a head needs no explanation. It cannot function and that's where we see a lot of people and ministries operating headless without that authority structure.

This should not be! Every person that lives on this earth, God's great big green earth, should be fathered. There are no exemptions; everyone is included. Being fathered means that you are covered, and you are counseled and prayed for and protected.

Do you know that, I don't do anything before I check with my fathers, in Heaven and the ones I have here on earth? When I receive counsel, I do my best to do what they say! You should receive wisdom from a multitude of counselors, that's more mature than you, so that you don't have to make the decision all by yourself.

Proverbs says, there is wisdom in a multitude of counsel. As a true and faithful believer, we must make sure that we position ourselves to receive that precious covering that the Lord has for us.

To receive a *spiritual father* should be as natural as anything spiritual and natural. If you are serving in a faithful church, submit to its authority. God is always faithful to lead you to someone that will father you and give you that precious covering. So, in this journey don't take on the mindset that you have to do it all alone with a rebel attitude.

That is not God's perfect plan. Choose and make that decision today to be covered in God's great chain of authority. I don't know the song but the title makes the point that in God's great kingdom, "You gotta serve somebody." I'm fathered by many fathers! You should be too.

Day 8: A Lesson From Grandpa Ford's Life

Have you read in Scripture the command, "Touch Not God's Anointed!" When I think of this statement, I remember the stance I saw my grandfather take toward my father. As you may know by now, in his season of life my father battled against alcohol. He made some very bad decisions that affected me and my whole family for the rest of our life.

I have spoken of the trespasses that were made against us many times. It altered my family's life. But this is the point, I would like to make this time. My grandfather, Grandpa Ford had a godly stance toward my father and his reverence to a holy God.

The act that almost took my mother's life had happened and all the family had to move back to Arkansas. My grandfather has always been known as the patriarch of the family—man that's in charge. And I mean that in a good way.

I always knew that my grandfather was no wimp, but in fact, a strongman, physically and spiritually. As a child, I remember thinking, what will Grandpa do about the great sin that was done to his youngest daughter, my mother? At that moment, I was concerned for a good while. I don't have too many memories of that time in my life.

But the memories I have, I remember very well and this one is very clear. My grandfather explained to me as a child that he couldn't touch my father in his trespass against his daughter. He told me that it was because he was a minister of God.

At that age, I could not understand everything he was saying. So, I just received what he said and listened. I was so young; I couldn't do anything, anyway. But now, that I'm older and have lived life for a while, I now understand. My grandfather was operating in the, 'Touch not my anointed' principle.

I know you may say, "Varn, how could you guys still honor your father after he caused so much pain and still respect him as a man of God?" I would say one name and it will explain it all, "Saul of Tarsus." We all know the call of God that was on his life.

If the Christians that he was persecuting had not forgiven him, his trespass against them, where would he be now in the scheme of things? He wouldn't be the great Apostle Paul that everybody knows. It took one of the faithful Christians to pray for him so that scales fell from his eyes so that he could see again. And they did pray for him. Do you see my point?

The main reason, I'm talking about this topic is to remind you, no matter what the trespass has been against you, we must forgive. I say this with much conviction, because I know there are some that have received much pain.

Yet, my confession is the same; we must forgive. The anointing demands it! Your story might be different than mine. My father was a Baptist minister with an alcoholic problem that ripped our family apart. But through forgiveness, there was healing and the pastoral ministry was restored to our family.

Through forgiveness and obedience to the Word of God, the anointing wasn't squelched! When we are obedient to the word of God, who knows what blessings and miracles may break out. So let's trust God's word and see!

Day 9: Three Common Mistakes Young Fathers Make

Young Fathers, here's three common mistakes men make in fulfilling the mission of fatherhood and how to heal them.

I want to encourage you as a young father. This is for fathers that have fallen short in the mission called fatherhood. I know you're there because I see you every day. You're my relatives, my friends, my friends' sons and my neighbors. And even more because, I've been there.

Let me tell you a little of my history. I became a young father in my mid-twenties. I loved being a father. There's nothing that I wouldn't do as a father, clean diapers or put my sons to sleep. I never let them out of my sight when they played outside.

Then there was the problem in my first marriage; we fought ninety percent of our seven-year marriage. Then the divorce and the separation from my sons almost killed me. But the Lord had mercy on me. I almost lost my mind.

It was the grace of the Lord that allowed me to keep our sons for the first two years after the breakup. Then they stayed with me every summer until they graduated high school. Now, the reason I'm telling you this story is so you can identify with my pain in this situation. In hopes, that you'll be able to receive my counsel in this matter for young fathers.

The Lord graced me to marry again. My wife and I did our best to be a good example of a good marriage before our sons. We have been married for twenty-three years at the time of this writing; praise the Lord.

Another reason, I speak about this matter is because I see this same scenario happening before me in the world and the church. I've prayed for many young fathers that are in this silent pain. Too many times, not only the woman but men are devoured in the situation called 'Divorced with Children.' They end up with no rights as a father. I wouldn't wish this pain on my worst enemy.

My desire is to help you avoid this pain. But since things are how they are, I want to give you my best counsel. Whether you find yourself divorced as a father or a single young man as a father, there are three common mistakes we as men make in fatherhood.

No forgiveness. The first thing you young fathers have to do is forgive yourself. Then forgive everyone else involved. Forgiveness is key; it opens the door to a new life. In this case, most of the young fathers may not have been fathered themselves. I know this is not the case, all the time; but it is usually that way.

No commitment. The second thing you need to do is still commit to be a good father to your children. Even, if it's only a small amount of time that you get to spend with your children, be the best you can be. I always told my sons; I only got fifteen minutes with my dad a year. And look how I turned out, I'm not that bad. And we would smile.

No patience. Third, decide to be present for the long haul. Many of us want to avoid pain. So, we end up not intentionally, but nevertheless, avoiding our children. Because every time, we see them it's a reminder of that pain.

I cried every time I had to put them on a plane back to their mom in another state. One time I was a little sick when I took them to the airport, after putting them on the plane and going back to my car I cried so hard; a stranger stopped and asked me if I was ok. By the time my youngest was in the twelfth grade, I think I stopped weeping, well I only had a few tears.

My point is I kept doing it. I kept sending for them. I kept facing the pain and walking it through (their pain and my pain). Just to encourage you; it does get better. I didn't mean to tell you such a sad story. But I do hope to prepare you, encourage and strengthen you. I will speak on this matter more in the future. So, stay encouraged.

Day 10: The Next Generation And A Bit Of Respect

First of all, if you haven't noticed by now, I'm a bit old school. I have a few concerns with the next generation and here is one of them. I'm from a family of brothers raised by my mother with one sister.

By us having a single parent, we had to do a lot of hard work for ourselves. You know, like cooking, cleaning, yard work and large gardens; that was all home work. The work that we did out of the home, me and my brothers, this work I saw them do and I did it too.

From my point of view, as youngsters we chopped cotton eight hours a day in full sun for six dollars a day all summer. I worked for the state forest department cutting trees with an axe in the deep woods. It was so hot I would stay wet from head to toe as a teenager.

I'm from a family of carpenters and if you know the work you're in full sun all day. I did carpentry work, almost half my life, framing, roofing, and siding work. As an adult, I've been an arborist for almost thirty years; I have trimmed thousands of trees that were over seventy feet tall and have cut down hundreds of five and six feet wide dead trees.

If you know tree work, you know hard work. So again, this is something I've done all my life and watched my brothers do right beside me. Now, here's my concerns with the next generation. I'm not calling names; I can but I won't, out of a dozen youngsters, I haven't seen but a few take up the challenge and follow suit.

I know from generation to generation, it should get better and smarter. But, even in this day hard work never killed anybody. I'm not saying that all are lazy because I see beautiful success in most of them. But I've seen a lot of boot scooting to avoid the hard stuff. Now, you may have wondered why father Varn is a bit indifferent.

That's one of the reasons. The next one is "respect." The reason I say this is I've seen men and fathers, in general, especially my brothers work hard and give out of a resource that they weren't given, in the first place. And it is beautiful in my sight. My hat's off to you men.

I saw the long hard hours you put in to provide for your family as best you could. I'm not the only that sees. Our Father God sees too. Sure, you weren't perfect. I'm not perfect and neither is anyone else. I always say, respect is earned! In my eyes, you've earned it. So, I encourage the upcoming generation, show some respect. It's long overdue.

Day 11: About Our Father's Business?

Are you faithfully serving in God's Kingdom? I believe every Christian should ask themselves these questions, like. When was the last time you personally led someone to the Lord?

Or have you ever led someone to the Lord? Are you a faithful church goer, and do you serve faithfully in your local church? Do you tithe and are you faithful in your tithing?

What type of fruit are you bearing, is it godly fruit? Finally, Jesus said that we should store up treasure in Heaven; what kind of treasure are you storing up in heaven. Will it be burned up or will it be an eternal reward, remaining there throughout eternity stored up for you.

The reason I ask these question, I see a lot of Christians by their confession they are, but when you wait to see the fruit, there aren't any to observe. I know that this can sound pretty tough but it's true. I know the word says that it's not by works that we are saved, but through grace.

It seems that some of us are using this as an excuse to wade through the water and that's it. This should not be! As a blood bought Christian, the price was paid and it was not cheap, It cost our Christ his life. As you may know by now he took it to the cross and gave it for us on Calvary.

This act alone has obligated us to take up the cross daily and follow after the Lord. This is the reason that I asked the question with this title. Are you faithfully, about our Father's business, that means day in and day out being his hands and feet consistently in serving our Lord and Savior.

I don't know, if I'm the only one that this is done to but all of my friends have always said to me, Varn, why don't you slow down and take a break, relax. Take a chill pill and let someone else do it for a while. They are speaking of being a witness for Christ.

I know I would give them this weird look. Because, I can't separate Christ and his power from who I am. I'm pretty sure I would just smile. My point is, I think everyone should be busy for the kingdom of God.

In all kinds of ways, in everything from A to Z in the kingdom of God, we have work to do. The days, we're living in are the last days. We must be about our Father's business for the day of the Lord cometh!

Day 12: The Fathering Spirit, I

Ya'll go sit down and be quiet while the Lord's doing his work! I have a funny but real story that brings fun memories to mind, when I think about it. Whenever it rains, thunders very hard and winds blow or it looks like Na-da weather, that's short in Arkansas for tornado weather; I look for a couch to sit on.

"I get somewhere and be very quiet, looking to see what color the wall's gonna turn this time." You know I borrowed that line from, "The Color Purple." Because that's the way it was in stormy seasons, when I was growing up.

Back in my younger days, when my family stayed with my Grandparents, I got to see a lot of old traditions. Some I understood and some I didn't. All I know is when we were told to do something, we did it. I remember about a dozen of them and here is one of them.

Whenever a big storm was brewing, my Grandfather, would point at the clouds and say, "A big one is coming." We would look at the clouds at the end of the day and talk about the weather it would bring the next day. Grandpa could look at the clouds and tell if it was going to be a sunny day or not.

We had this very large field in front of our house, so we could see the clouds coming out of the southwest. We were in central Arkansas. There would be very large storms that blew in from that direction. Some were big enough to put you on your knees to pray.

My grandparents had a tradition, whenever it began to thunder and lightning a lot, they would cut off all electric things like the T.V and the Radio. They would tell all us children to go and sit down on the couch.

They would say, "Be quiet while the Lord is doing his work." And we would do it! Thinking back on those moments, I cherish those times because I learned to know and reverence the Lord.

At this my heart pounds and leaps from its place. Listen! Listen to the roar of his voice, to the rumbling that comes from his mouth. He unleashes his lighting beneath the whole heaven and sends it to the ends of the whole earth.

After that comes the sounds of his roar; he thunders with his majestic voice. When his voice resounds, he holds nothing back. God's voice thunders in marvelous ways; he does great things beyond our understanding.

He says to the snow, "Fall on earth, and to the rain shower, "Be a mighty down pour." So that all men he has made may know his work, he stops every man from his labor. — Job 37:1-7

I believe this is where my grandparents got their word of God from.

Day 13: The Fathering Spirit, II

As I was saying Mama said, "Ya'll go sit down and be quiet while the Lord's doing his work!" During that season, I was probably about ten or thirteen. Years later, when I had become an adult I was living in Dallas and was a tree arborist by trade. My brothers and I were all tree experts.

Once my mother came to visit her sons and daughter. As usual she would go to every son's house, stay and visit all the grandkids. This time we were all at my big brother's house because he had the pool. We were having fun with the whole family in fellowship.

All of a sudden a storm came up and it seemed to be a bad one. So we all ran for cover. Mom, the patriarch of the family, looked at the whole group of us and said, "You guys need to settle down and be quiet. Let the Lord do his work."

Now before I tell you who put his foot in his mouth I want to say, I have always been a good and respectful son to my mother. But I guess I got the big head and lost my mind for a moment and said something like, "Mom that's an old tradition, we'll be o.k. this time."

What did I say that for? All hell broke loose; the tornados came from everywhere. The electricity went out; the wind was blowing and stuff flying everywhere. When we got up the next morning, it was like a bomb had gone off.

In the Spring time, it was normal that the tree business went crazy, when all the storms come through. We had never seen anything like that before. As a tree expert, I specialize in taking very large trees off of houses without a crane.

That season, we took off many with cranes. A lot of the fallen and storm damaged trees were seventy feet tall and the trunks were five and six feet wide. We worked hard for weeks.

You can be sure I learned my lesson that day. One of the lessons was, "Just because our elders are older and have old fashioned traditions that don't make much sense to us now. It doesn't mean that they aren't a truth from the word of God.

So the moral of my story is, the next time you see or hear a storm coming and an elder says to you, "Sit down and be quiet." Do it!

Day 14: Father God And His Loving Chastisement, I

It's God's loving chastisement. Remember the writer of Isaiah proclaimed, "But he was wounded for our transgressions; he was bruised for our iniquities: the chastisement of our peace was upon him; and with his stripes we are healed. —Isaiah 53: 5-6

Today, I would like to talk about God's chastisement. The word of God says he chastises the one he loves, and that if he doesn't we are not his children. If we are not his children, then we are illegitimate. And who wants to be that.

I must be truthful to you about this matter; it seems to me that I'm always in the shed taking my paddling about something or some situation. I know that perception can be a bit awkward, but I'm working on that one.

My personality is an A type person or some call it a Mover. I'm usually right there in the face of the moment spouting out my opinions about any situation. Like Peter saying "Thou are the Christ," and the next moment saying, "No, Lord you can't go to Jerusalem where they kill the prophets." And Jesus having to say to him, "Satan, get thee behind me."

Meaning, we must be careful because bitter and sweet water shouldn't flow from the same vessel. I have enough courage to admit sometimes I put my foot in my mouth. And in that action of Peter, I could follow suit so I do my best to be careful.

That's where God steps in our lives and does the correcting. He does it the same way a good parent would do. A good parent chastises his children in love and compassion. Do you see it! The writer of Deuteronomy confirms this, "Thou shalt also consider in thine heart, that, as a man chastise his son, so the Lord chasteneth thee." — Deuteronomy 8:5

It seems to me that in this time, everybody wants to be right and no one is wrong and in need of correction. That's why this message isn't spoken about a lot; because the flesh doesn't want to be wrong.

But God holds that key to our lives in a matter of speaking, whether we are right or wrong. When we are right, we are blessed; when we are wrong he deals with us as a faithful father.

I find myself when I am disciplined by the Lord, my reactions are: I do the search first to see if I have done something wrong or not. Then I get quiet and yield to the process. I will admit that I do a good amount of squirming but I eventually submit to the process.

Now the question comes to you. Do you submit or do you play the rebel?

For instance, when David and Bathsheba did what they did, God sent the prophet to David and told him a story about the man and his flock of sheep.

He said instead of the man using his own sheep, he took his servant's little ewe lamb and made feast with it. It was revealed by the man of God that he (speaking of David) was the man that had sinned by taking another man's wife and committing adultery and murder.

Do you remember his reaction? Did David submit or did he yield to the discipline process of the Lord and the man of God? His reaction, he fell to the floor and said I am the man. And David said, "Will I die?"

The man of God said, "You shall not die but here are the consequences." It's the same with us and our sin. We may not repent until we're found out either. So, don't be too hard on David. The thing to remember is there were consequences to help him remember not to ever go that route again.

Day 15: Father God And His Loving Chastisement, II

As the story goes, God chastised him and declared that trouble would come against him out of his own household and the sword would never leave him. David bowed and worshiped and said Lord, let your will be done. —II Samuel 11

Now I have to say to you, I'm not in this just for the pain. But I am thankful for God's process of keeping us.

Read this, "Yet it pleased the Lord to bruise him; he hath put him to grief: when thou shalt make his soul an offering for sin, he shall see his seed, he shall prolong his days, and the pleasure of the Lord shall prosper in his hand." —Isaiah 53:10

This is the great mystery of God and His great Salvation for mankind. We humanity are still receiving understanding of this great and precious salvation.

Here's another one, "Now no chastisement for the presents seemeth to be joyous, but grievous: nevertheless, afterward it yieldeth the peaceable fruit of righteousness unto them which are exercised thereby." —Hebrews: 12:11.

Our heavenly Father knows his children and he knows what we need. When the Lord assigns us for a season of chastisement, He knows the process it will take and the fruit it will bring forth and bear.

In my own words, "I would rather get a whippin from the Lord, than to miss those pearly gates."

Many years ago when I first received Jesus as Lord and Savior in 1983, I was doing my best to try to enter into ministry by living a good Christian life. I would go and preach where ever the door was open for me to preach. Once I was talking to my uncle who is a pillar of our community and a Pastor of two Baptist churches.

I asked him a question. I guess I was trying to show him my maturity by the question that I would ask. Even while asking, I thought I knew the answer I said, "Uncle what happens if you are saved, backslide and go back to the world? Would you go to hell when you die if you didn't repent or would you still be saved?"

I'm pretty sure I looked at him with a look saying, I got you! Because I believed at that time in my life that you could sin to the point of losing your salvation. My Uncle looked at me with a father look because he was a father to me and said, "No, you won't lose your salvation, if you sin or run to far, the lord will whip you."

And after thirty years of serving the Lord, I think I bout got it figured out. Knowing and trusting in a faithful God!

One more, the writer of Proverbs 20:30 says, "By the wounds of the rod evil is taken away, and blows make clean the deep."

Day 16: Are We True Sons And Daughters?

Are we true sons and daughters or are we illegitimate? Now, I will start with saying please forgive me for being so harsh with my title. I promise I'm not saying all this for shock value. My heart is to make a point and for you to see the difference between the two. In the kingdom of God, we either are or we aren't true sons. The definition for bastard is, a person without a father's covering.

The word of God tells us. Do not despise God's discipline, his chastisement, for if you are a true son he will chastise you. I want you to think about this statement really good. If you are not being disciplined by our heavenly father you are not his child. I know you will say to me, how can God discipline me. I will say this, if you are his son you will truly find out.

Do not despise God's discipline. A true son will submit to God's chastisement, but an illegitimate one will flee or resist. This act in being disciplined, I can relate because I was raised by a single mother. She did her job very well making sure all her six kids turned out well. She had no problem disciplining us well.

That's why neither of us got in any major trouble because we knew that we would have hell to pay if we did. In Madear's voice! As you know, any good father has no problem in disciplining as well. So, how much more our heavenly father is toward us his children.

My wife and I have entered a season where the Lord has been disciplining us. The natural response is to say to the Lord, why me! What did I do wrong? And we did for a good season ask that question. After submitting to the process and allowing our heavenly father to get our full attention, this revelation came to my wife and we discussed it.

This is what came to us. A true son submits and doesn't flee from the process nor does he despise the chastisement. He or she allows the Lord to complete the task and receive the process by faith. An illegitimate person would rebel and flee, yielding to impatience and pride, like the first reaction of the prodigal son.

Day 17: Are We True Sons And Daughters, II

And you have forgotten that word of encouragement that addresses you as sons: "My sons, do not make light of the Lord's discipline, and do not lose heart when he rebukes you, because the Lord disciplines those he loves, and he punishes everyone he accepts as a son." —Hebrews 12:5-11

Endure hardship as discipline; God is treating you as sons. For what son is not disciplined by his father? If you are not disciplined (and everyone undergoes discipline), then you are illegitimate, children and not true sons. Moreover, we have all had human fathers who disciplined us and we respected them for it.

How much more should we submit to the father of our spirits and live. Our father disciplined us for a little while as they thought it best; but God disciplined us for our good, that we may share in his holiness. No discipline seems pleasant at the time, but painful. Later on, however, it produces a harvest of righteousness and peace for those who have been trained by it.

So we see that chastisement is not itself only for punishment alone, but for correction to maturity and growth.

In Romans 8:14, "Those who are led by the spirit of God are the sons of God. For you did not receive a spirit that makes you a slave again to fear, but you received the spirit of sonship. And by him we cry, 'Abba Father.'" The Spirit himself testifies with our spirit that we are God's children. Now, if we are children, then we are heirs— heirs of God and co-heirs with Christ, if indeed we share in his sufferings in order that we may, also, share in his glory.

And again, the Galatian writer instructs about sonship, "Because you are sons, God sent his Spirit of his son into our hearts, the Spirit who calls out, "Abba Father." So you no longer are a slave, but a son; and since you are a son, God has made you an heir." —Galatians 4:6

The beautiful thing about all this is it's in Gods Holy plan, he has made it that we share in his glory. He planned it that we share in our Christ suffering and in that we are his beloved sons and daughters. And since we joined him in his suffering as sons and daughters, we became heirs, and as heirs in Christ we also reign in his Glory to live with him forever.

Day 18: Encouraging Young Fathers, II

I want to make a point about the role of the father. I am one, I am a son of my father; I have become a grandfather. God has graced every man with the ability to become a father. Yet, there is a great responsibility that comes with the position.

The best we can do is be the best we can be through the grace of God and his word. There are no perfect fathers. My intentions were to be the best father that I could be. I feel I did pretty good. On the other hand, in some areas I'm sure I failed miserably.

All you have to do is ask your children; they will tell you. Here comes my point. But, you have to be careful, because in my case; I really didn't have a father. Or I could say barely had. God blessed me to pour out of a vessel that hadn't been poured into. The reason I say this is because I've seen men give from a place where they hadn't received themselves as fathers.

Then I see the grown children of that father want to disrespect that same father for not giving more. Where is the shame? The one that gave from nothing or the one that received a little more because he was given a little more.

Do you know that we have a God that looks at each situation forensically? Meaning, our God is not a man that he should lie. He doesn't look at situations and go by the "he-say-she-say."

If you've been a good father but made some mistakes and you tried your best. You are still a good father in God's eyes. This principle holds true; before the accuser can say anything, it still applies. We must take the log out of our own eye before we can remove the twig out of the other person's eye.

Now, I know there are some bad fathers and mothers out there. I'm not talking about those now. I'm only talking about the good ones. The reason I mentioned this is because I see it happening in many young fathers' life.

As for the sons of these fathers, after they receive their children they seem to get this chip on their shoulder saying, I'm going to do better than you did for me. My advice is don't be so quick to be the critic and judge. The word of God is true; become the judge and you're likely to be judged with the same measuring tape. Life will be the teacher!

The truth is, they should do better because they were given more! But it must be in the utmost respect, toward their parents. My fear is for a generation that's not giving respect, there could be spiritual repercussions and I don't say this lightly.

Need a reference, read the life of King David's life. So, if you are a Dad, be the very best you can be and leave the rest up to God's holy judgement and forensics. He knows what to do on this matter.

Day 19: Ten Things I would Tell Myself As A Young Father, I

Have you ever wished you could have 'the talk' with your younger self? You know the one that made all kinds of mistakes because no one told him or the times he didn't listen. I'm not just talking about the birds and bees talk but about life, in general, things that will make your life go better.

Well, you can now benefit from 'the talk' I would have with my younger-self. Here are the ten things I would tell myself as a young father.

The reason I'm speaking on these things is because I didn't have them spoken to me when I was your age. There are two most important decisions that you will make in your life. The first will be, making Jesus Lord and Savior of your life. The next will be who you marry.

Because when you marry, you will become one in yourselves, before the Lord. So, young man and young lady choose well. You will live with the good decision you make for the rest of your life.

1. As a young father, it is very important to make sure Jesus is Lord of your life. There is great counsel in the word of God. You can only receive its revelation, if you are born again. By God being the ruler of your life, the Lord can lead you and help you to raise your family by his Spirit. In a life of faith and trust, you can make a beautiful family.

2. You must be filled with the Spirit of God. Make sure that you are baptized in the Holy Spirit. When you are filled with the Holy Spirit, you will see a change; it will be as different as night is from day. The Holy Spirit will give you power like you've never seen before. You will be able to say yes, when you need to say yes and no to the things that you need to say no to. When I received the baptism of the Holy Spirit, my life changed forever and I was filled with power to do the Lord's will.

3. Love your wife and family as Christ loved the church and gave his life for it. If you have a wife, remember we (the body of Christ) are the bride and Christ is the groom. A marriage is a type of relationship as Christ is to the church. We should treat our wives, likewise. Love your wife as Christ has loved the church. Family should be in its rightful place; the kingdom of God is all about the family. Be blessed young fathers!

Money, Hard Work And Good Priorities

4. I would tell myself about money: You know moolah, greenbacks, dough... As a young father, I would like to have known more about how to manage my money better. I must say it was mostly my fault not paying enough attention in the class room. I'm doing much better.

But I lost a lot of precious time I could've spent saving. The Lord has graced me to have a good life graced with self-control and not having a life style running all over the place, "doing Lord knows what."

My advice to you is to implement a good plan in your finances. Make sure you start saving early and spend your money wisely. Oh yes, I married an accountant which helps.

5. Then there's hard work. I would tell myself how valuable hard work is. I know you're probably saying, hard work? Yes, hard work is very good for you. Here's why, it becomes an advantage country boys have on the city boys. If you were raised in the country, you will have to work. I've done jobs with city friends that have never worked hard.

A few have looked at me and said, "Varn I don't do this kind of work." That would always puzzle me. Work will help establish you as a man. You will always feel complete after a job that's been done well.

Work your best and don't ever be afraid or ashamed of hard work. There are benefits that are unseen in the process of hard work. For one thing, God sees, rewards and promotes. I've worked many hard jobs. I've met few that could keep up with me.

Day 20: Ten Things I would Tell Myself As A Young Father, II

6. Make good priorities. In this priority list, there should be God first, wife, family, job, church. Honor God; if the Lord is honored first, then all else will fall into place. The word of God says, 'Seek ye first the kingdom of God and all will be added to you.' We must allow the Lord to be Lord over our families.

Family should be in its rightful place in your priorities. The kingdom of God is all about the family. Abraham, Isaac, and Jacob. It is Gods desire that the blessings of God be passed down to the third, fourth, fifth generations and beyond.

Finally, your job or work represent the kings of the kingdom. Your household and the church can't operate without the kings in the house. The first main priority for a man is to have a job and to provide for his family. If you're not, you are falling short.

For most men, it is an honor to provide for their family. It should be for you too. Church still is very important; you must make sure you and your family attend a spirit filled church that teaches the word of God and the baptism of the Holy Spirit.

Church, Giving, Going Deeper With God And Fatherhood

7. Speaking of church, this is worth repeating, it is very important to make sure that you and your family are involved in a good word Church. Just any church won't do. It is important to go to a good word church, a church that believes and teaches the whole word of God. You, the young father must make sure that the word of God is being preached there.

Remember, the word of God says, my people perish for the lack of knowledge. Make sure that your family doesn't perish. Young father be involved with your family in church and thank him for gracing you with such a beautiful family. There are plenty of people that will tell you, everyone is not so fortunate.

8. You should be a giver. There are different ways that you can give to the Lord. The first I will talk to you about is, tithing. If not already, become a tither. Yes, it means giving ten percent of your earnings according to Malachi 3:10, so that the house of God would have provision.

I recently wrote an article on this topic: In Tithes & Offerings. Everyone doesn't have the faith to tithe. Even though, we should a lot of people don't. Some say they love God but they don't have the faith to give him ten percent and trust him with the ninety percent that's left. What's up with that?

As an older me, I would tell my younger self, trust God with all your heart and trust him with your finances, too. The word of God says in Malachi that the Lord would look down from Heaven and pour you out so much blessing that you would have to give some away.

Now that's what I desire. And the Lord will rebuke the devourer for your sake. And your vine will not discard its fruit before it's time. It takes faith to tithe but it's worth it.

Serving in the kingdom of God is an additional way to give. I recommend volunteering in the church at every age and level. When you take care of God's business he will definitely take care of yours. Serving is the first step in ministering before the Lord. If someone says to you they want to be a minister. The first thing you should see is them volunteering in the church before the Lord.

Day 21: Ten Things I would Tell Myself As A Young Father, III

9. You should seek to go deeper with God. The first experience in the Lord is being born again which is very important. Jesus said it's not the most important to be able to cast out devils. The most important is that your name is written in the Lamb's book of Life. The next very important thing is to be baptized in the (Holy Ghost) aka Holy Spirit.

The writer of the book of Acts tells us, Paul was traveling down the coast until he reached Ephesus and came upon some of John the Baptist disciples and asked them if they had received the baptism of the Holy Spirit. They said, no we hadn't even heard of the Holy Spirit.

He asked them, what have you received then? They said, only the baptism that John the Baptist preached a baptism of repentance. So Paul laid hands on them and they received the Holy Spirit and were filled and spoke in tongues and prophesied. Acts 19

I mentioned going deeper, because in the Lord, deep calls unto deep. Here's a quick testimony. I had served the Lord for about five or six years. Now I personally believe one of the reasons this happened to me is because I was ordained to be a part of the five-fold ministry. I'm telling you this because this may be your word.

In this season of my life, I was serving in the jail and prison ministry. We would go to the halfway house where inmates came after they were released from prison.

We had services every Thursday night for the men. We would bring them food and the word of God. We would have a service of the word, worship and ministry.

Here's where my deeper came in. After each service, we would talk and pray with the men individually in a time of ministry. In this season, every time I would take a person to minister to them, I would pray for them to be filled with the Holy Spirit and they would be filled. Laughing, crying, and praying in tongues, all at the same time.

During that season, the Lord spoke to me in a dream and said to me, "Varn, if you keep praying with the men and helping them receive the baptism in the Holy Spirit, in six months, I will promote you.

I took it as a word of the Lord and made sure that I stayed faithful for the next six months. One thing I learned that when God speaks of promotion, it's usually not what we think.

The promotion did come. One Sunday morning at church about six months later, I was sitting on a front pew with my wife, she was to my right. My mother was to my left and my leader, Mrs. Inga Davis was to her left. We were a part of the Be Free Ministry.

The fire of God fell upon me, at that moment, it was like a hot coal from heaven was sat upon me. It seems like, for about an hour, though I'm sure it was only about twenty or thirty minutes.

I felt like if I would move I would die. A ministry mantle fell upon me that day and still rest upon me to this day. From that day, I would never be the same.

So, my advice to my younger self and to you is to keep going and stay faithful for there is more for you in God. He's calling you deep. "Deep calls unto deep…" Isaiah 6:5-7

10. Make a decision to make sure you are being fathered and receive your father by faith. So, are you fathered? This is an important question. It is very important if you want to fulfil the Lord's will in your Life. You may say, Varn, I have no father or my father is dead.

Or I don't know my father and yes, some of you may be saying, I don't want to know my father. You know I could go on but wherever you are with that question, Gods got you covered. I mean literally! God wants to be your Father.

If you have or had a good father that is awesome. There is a responsibility that comes with that blessing. Remember, 'to much is given, much is required.' But to the fatherless, God wants you covered. There are spiritual fathers that the Lord has sent us, some are pastors, teachers, coaches, deacons, step fathers, grandpas, etc.

The Lord has spiritual fathers that are filled with the Spirit of God and are led by the Holy Spirit. They are willing and obedient to do the Father's will in being a father to you.

God said, he would be a father to the fatherless. If you feel abandoned and you feel you are fatherless, just say a simple prayer and ask Father God to be your father. You might even find out he's already answered before you asked.

It happened like that for me. I received all kinds of fathers and mentors in my life. In any case, the Lord will hear you. His fathering spirit will cover you. It is the Lord's will that we are covered, mentored, watched over, loved, rebuked and even chastised. Those are the duties of a father. Now the ball is in your court. All you have to do is by faith receive yours today.

Day 22: The Prodigal Son

There was a father and he had two sons. One day one of the sons came to him and said father it's time for me to leave. I think I've been here long enough. It's time for me to see the world. Can I have my portion of the family's money that's coming to me? The father said to him, son I don't think you're ready but if you insist, I will not stop you.

So, the son leaves and goes to the big city and does what he believes he's been missing. He partied, stayed out all night, got drunk, became sexually promiscuous and spent all his money with his friends at the casino.

The son left prematurely and soon saw that his money was running out. So, he says to himself, I can call my friends that I partied with; surely they'll give me a helping hand before I run out of money.

He started calling all his numbers that he had but he only got voicemail. Then he began to text everyone and every one responded and said things like, man I'm broke too or who did you say this was? We did what together? Man don't text me again.

The very next day our nation went to war and our nation's economy went south and there was no work to be found. He said to himself again, 'self you are in big trouble.' Hard times had caught up with him. He had no place to work, no place to live and no one to call to help him.

So, he hired himself out to work at the only place he could find, a hog farm. His one and only job was to slop the hogs. One day he was so disgusted with himself because he found himself staring at the husk of rotten corn that he was feeding to the hogs and about to put it in his mouth; he was so hungry.

After sitting and crying his eyes out and cussing like three sailors, he stopped and thought to himself, "I must be crazy. I will go back to my father's house!"

He said "I've seen them punching the time clock and picking up their check on Friday. Cashing that check and getting groceries on the way home. Speaking of groceries, he started thinking of all the things they probably bought at the grocery store. My father's employees are much better off than me." I will go and say, "Father, I have sinned against you and God, I'm sorry, please hire me back as a general worker. I will work for you. I will gladly be an assistant to whoever you assign me to!"

As for the father, he is doing like he has been doing ever since the first day his son left, sitting on his front porch saying to himself, maybe today my son will come back home. With a twist of his ring on his finger, he anticipates what he will say when his son comes home.

Thinking out loud, he says I will give him this ring of my own authority. Not only that but I've already bought the suits that I'm going to give him. Of course, I've hung a nice coat in his closet waiting for him. I know he's been cold.

The dinner party is already arranged. The robo-calls are set up to call everyone with the good news and inviting them to the celebration. I'm gonna throw him one big party. The father has rehearsed this scene, many times, over and over in his mind and out loud.

Then one early morning, the father was sitting on the porch and his son's dog Hougy gave a loud bark, all of a sudden, and took off like a rocket. As he watched the dog run down the road, he knew that it had to be his son that was coming. Before he could actually see him, the father took out, right after the dog.

The father saw him and ran to meet his son. When he got to him, even before the son got to make his confession to the father as he still had plans to do. The father fell upon his neck and kissed him repeatedly. He told him that he loved and missed him and was waiting on him to come.

The son started out telling the father how sorry he was; how he had sinned against God and against him. He even got out how he was willing to be hired help...But that was as far as he got. His father put his hand to his lips and said, no more, this is what I'm going to do.

When he got back to the house he shouted to everyone and said. "Hey everyone, my son that was lost has come home, come and celebrate with me!" Before all the people, the father kissed his son again, he placed his signet ring of authority on him and gave him his new suits and reminded him he was covered. Then the father said, let's throw a party because my son has returned.

The son that stayed at home and was faithful in all his father business, lacked one thing. He wasn't all that happy at his brother's return. He said to himself.

My father didn't make a great feast for me. Nor have I received any ring or suits. How can he do this for that brother of mine who has run off and squandered all our living. He's not even given me a little party.

So, he was offended and did not attend. The father said to his offended son, you have been with me all this time. My provision has always been there for you. If you wanted new suits, I would have ordered them for you.

If you wanted to throw a party, all you had to do was ask. Son, you are my faithful son. My favor has always been with you! Won't you come and celebrate with me. "Because your brother that was lost has now come home."

Day 23: Why Father God?

Do you know why our God is called Father God? It's because he fathers us! We have all had fathers that did their best to give us the best for ourselves. So how much more will our heavenly father know what to do for us.

We've briefly discussed this before. There is such a thing as God's loving chastisement. Do you know that by you being a child of God, He will not allow you to get away with what others get away with? And the reason for that is, you are His beloved sons and daughters.

When I was young, my mother would take the belt to me, whenever I got out of line. And I can say, most of the time, I knew I deserved it. So, in the same loving spirit, the Lord chastises us. You can be sure of it, if you are acting up he will have at it!

So, this is what I have to say. Stop trying to save your brothers and sisters when the Lord is doing his work. You keep interfering and you just might get in on it, too. I remember my mother saying, boy move your hands. I kept trying to put my hands up to stop the belt from hitting me. So, it's best children of God, be an obedient child of God and mind your own business.

For whom the Lord loves He chastens, and scourges every son whom He receives. If you endure chastening, God deals with you as with sons; for what son is there whom a father does not chasten? But if you are without chastening, of which all have become partakers, then you are illegitimate and not sons.

Furthermore, we have had human fathers who corrected us, and we paid them respect. Shall we not much more readily be in subjection to the Father of spirits and live?

For they indeed for a few days chastened us as seemed best to them, but He for our profit, that we may be partakers of His holiness. Now no chastening seems to be joyful for the present, but painful; nevertheless, afterward it yields the peaceable fruit of righteousness to those who have been trained by it. —Hebrews 12:6-11

Day 24: Words That Shouldn't Be In Your Vocabulary

I must confess I really don't want to speak on this subject but it keeps coming before me. I must obey the Holy Spirit. So, here we go! I see a few people that profess that they are Christian. And I believe them; some I've even gone to church with at different points in my life.

There is this word that I see used; it's a known word from my old unsaved days. It is an unclean word. It should not be used by anyone that's been bought by so great of a price.

The word is -- I can't say it and it really hurts even when I think it. It is WT*. Now I hate that I even have to mention it but it's needful. Those letters are the first alphabet of each word but I can't say the last one. This word was birthed out of the pits of hell. It should never be used by a Christian.

If a Christian uses this word it makes me wonder if they are truly born again. And most definitely not baptized in the Holy Ghost. The Spirit of God wouldn't let you say that. He would convict you so bad, you wouldn't be able to get from off the floor.

I'm really being polite from what I really want to say. So, I will end this before I get into some trouble. Here's a scripture reference:

Do not let any unwholesome talk come out of your mouths but only what is helpful for building others up according to their needs, that it may benefit those who listen. —Ephesians 4: 29

O.k., one more just in case, you need convincing.

And now, dear brothers and sisters, one final thing. Fix your thoughts on what is true, and honorable, and right, and pure, and lovely, and admirable. Think about things that are excellent and worthy of praise. — Philippians 4:8

And do not grieve the Holy Spirit, with whom you were sealed for the Day of Redemption. So if you have used this word in your vocabulary, repent and ask the Lord to forgive you. And He will graciously do it.

Day 25: Spiritual Fathers, I

In these last days, before the Lord comes, there is a great need for fathers. It is very evident, especially, among African Americans. Yes, I am one of them that was in great need. But, by the grace of God, I have received many 'spiritual fathers' by now.

Yet, there's not a day that goes by that I don't see the need in someone's life. Every place my wife and I go, we see the need for fathers, physical and spiritual. We may watch a movie and see it. We turn to each other both saying, "It's a father story!

Or he or she has a 'father wound.' Looking at the news, we both say, "there's another father need.' A lot of what's going on in the world, can truly be traced back to the effect of the father need or what we've been calling the father wound.

We Need You – Fathers!

Here's one of the reasons, I can say this with conviction. The statistics are there for all to see that we need a God intervention. And the Lord has given us a solution, it's called 'spiritual fathers.'

Father Related Statistics
- 63% of youth suicides are from fatherless homes – 5 times the average.
- 90% of all homeless and runaway children are from fatherless homes – 32 times the average.
- 85% of all children who show behavior disorders come from fatherless homes – 20 times the average.
- 80% of rapists with anger problems come from fatherless homes –14 times the average.
- 71% of all high school dropouts come from fatherless homes – 9 times the average.

Father Factor in Education
- Fatherless children are twice as likely to drop out of school.

- Children with Fathers who are involved are 40% less likely to repeat a grade in school.
- Children with Fathers who are involved are 70% less likely to drop out of school.
- Children with Fathers who are involved are more likely to get A's in school.
- Children with Fathers who are involved are more likely to enjoy school and engage in extracurricular activities.

Now, I do want to say that there are beautiful fathers out there. And I want to give them all a big enormous shout out, for doing a great job! Hooah! Hooah!

But as you already know, there's not enough, that's why there is a call for more spiritual fathers.

Day 26: Spiritual Fathers, II

You are qualified, if you are filled with the spirit of God, love the word of God and doing your best to be led by the Holy Spirit. You are a candidate, if you are mature in the faith and you know how to walk in love and forgiveness.

You are an obedient son of God. I didn't say perfect, just being willing to continue growing and quick to repent when you mess up makes you a perfect choice to become the spiritual father, the sons and daughters in your sphere of influence need.

The word of God says, in the last days, I will pour out my Spirit upon all flesh, and your sons and daughters will prophesy. — Acts 2:17

The Lord is positioning us for a move of God. Can you picture it? It is happening, even as we speak. There's a generation that's being raised up that is calling forth the will of God. We all will benefit from it.

If you are feeling the call to be a father to many, if not already, position yourself to be used by our heavenly Father to become a 'Spiritual Father.' Yes, it's just that easy, just make yourself available and the Lord will use you.

I'm so excited about this because the Lord used my Grandfather to help raise me as a spiritual and physical father. He was just what our family needed, at the right time. And the Lord wants to use us in the same manner.

Are You In Need Of One?

Now, don't feel bad about it, I rowed in that same boat, too, for way too long. "Don't be scared," the Lord will be faithful to you, just like he was with me. The reason I say this is because, "The heavenly Father" is just that, a Father and it matters to him. As a son, we must only position ourselves to be able to receive, by faith.

Now, you can't go in there with a guns-blazing attitude. There must be a humbling of yourself. Remember, you are the one as a son with the need. So let that, be a motivation for you. Do like I did, and receive many spiritual fathers.

A Father's Gift

Every good gift and every perfect gift is from above, coming down from the Father of lights with whom there is no variation or shadow due to change. —James 1:17

Remember this, our Father God wants us to have good success. It is his perfect will that we accomplish a successful life and mentor others to do the same. It is easier with having fathers. One of the reasons why it's such a need, you see, a father has already been there, where you are headed. He can pull from his experience, wisdom and help give you good directions.

He'll be like, do it this way, or you may can try it that way. Then he's like, "Oh no!" don't do it that way, it won't work. I've made that big mistake before. The lessons will be priceless for a next generation.

So, make sure that you ask God for a spiritual father in your life. Like me, you'll probably begin to see God has already sent many, you didn't recognize in the past. And the good thing about this is, you can have more than one.

Receive your spiritual fathers then turn and become the father someone else needs. You're doing it already! I have faith in you. This is God's perfect will for you, keep it going. I declare today, "I'm no longer fatherless!"

Day 27: Fathers Interfere

In ancient days, there was a father and son. The father was so busy in the military; he never had time to interfere or even tell him no, about anything. The father was a king of a nation. The son was a prince and his name was Adonijah. He was the brother of Absalom.

They were both princes, spoiled and very good looking. The Bible says that his brother Absalom hair was so long, that he suffered from neck strain a lot because his hair was too heavy for him to carry around.

Again, they both had the same family problem. They were very spoiled and their father had no time to rebuke or reprove them. He was so busy fighting wars and ruling his kingdom. Since that was the situation, Adonijah, as a young man, came up with this crazy idea.

By this time, their father was old and nearing the end of his life. In fact, it was almost time for the kingdom to change hands from father to son, but no son had been named yet. Of course, they all knew that it had been prophesied that the kingdom would go to King David's son, Solomon.

Well, Adonijah still had this dumb idea that he should be the new king, without his father's appointment. So, he went and got himself fifty men to run ahead of him and rode in his chariot with his horses pulling him. He started his own parade and proclaimed himself king.

But there was one very big problem. Just a few hours later, his father the King anointed his brother Solomon, as the new and true king. As Adonijah was in his arranged party celebrating with his paid people to be there, they began to hear a clamber of loud noise. They asked themselves, what is this?

Someone came in and said, King David just anointed, Solomon as King! That is the noise you are hearing. Adonijah panicked; ran in fear and took hold to the horns of the Altar, fearing for his life. He said, go and tell Solomon that I won't come down unless he promises me that he won't kill me.

King Solomon sent word to him and said, if there is no treachery found in you, no harm will come to you. But if treachery is found, you will, surely die.

Adonijah said, 'ok, I agree to your terms. And Solomon told him to go home.

Now you tell me, what do you think, eventually, happened to Solomon's half-brother Adonijah and his rebellion?

According to Scripture, this is what happened. Because he was not interfered with (he was never told no), he never turned from his rebellious ways. He, eventually, tried again to take the kingdom through deception and espionage. King Solomon had already warned him but he didn't listen. He paid for it with his life. My point is, it didn't have to happen that way.

There was enough provision for Adonijah to rule in his own delegated authority. But I guess that wasn't enough for him. So, the moral of this story is, fathers interfere with your children. Tell them no every now and then, lest they have a similar fate.

For more teaching on this topic, get a copy of Varn's upcoming book 'The Character Of King David." For a free sample chapter – David, The Warrior, visit varnbrown.com.

Day 28: Grandpa Ford A God Man

My grandfather was a God man. He lived the best life he could in Christ. My Pastor is a God man. King David was a God man; Elijah was a God man, Ruth was a God man, Esther was a God man. When I ask the question, are you a God man? I'm not only speaking about the male species, but humanity!

These are the words that you don't want said to you, if you are a God man, "stand away from me for I never knew you." As a God man, I do my best to live my life congruently by the word of God so that I don't hear those words.

Not everyone who says to me Lord, Lord, will enter the kingdom of heaven but only he who does the will of my Father who is in heaven. – Matthew 7:21

Many will say to me on that day Lord, Lord, did we not prophesy in your name, and in your name drive out demons and perform many miracles? Then I will plainly say, I never knew you, away from me you evil doers.

The Lord did not know them in the body of Christ. As you know, intimacy means: very close or familiar. "In-to-me-see," is the way I say it. He did not know their works or their fruit was not congruent to his word.

This fear of the Lord "keeps me" fear of his judgment and a godly fear of falling short. I believe humanity needs a large dose of godly reverential fear. This scripture Matthew 7:21 above does that for me.

You know when you accept Jesus and agree to follow Him, you are in covenant with our Lord. You may know already, a covenant is an agreement, compact, to promise by a covenant, to make a covenant.

So, this covenant is a promise between you and the heavenly Father. You promise the Lord that you will serve him faithfully and follow after him hard and do your best to obey his word.

And in return, the Lord says that he will cover you and hide you under his wings, shelter you, protect you and your house in his mighty fortress. When your enemies attack you and get strong against you, He will give them trouble all of their own.

I've said in my writing that a Christian should always check themselves; this is really one of those times. We should examine ourselves before the Lord has to do it.

For on that last and final day God will and by then it will be too late. So we should all do the things of obedience more and more. We should keep watch over and judge ourselves, too, with the Holy Spirit's help. You know, along with praying and doing the work of Christ while it is still day.

Now, I look at this situation of the fruit of the people. They felt they were doing pretty good. They told Him they had prophesied in His name, cast out devils and preformed miracles. If you look at the Church, the body of Christ today. I mean all denominations, Baptist, Catholic, Church of God in Christ and Pentecostal, etc. Most of those churches believe and do those works they mention prophesy, cast out devils and miracles.

But with these people the Lord described in Scripture with their works, he had to say, "Away from me! I never knew you." It was because of their disobedience. It could be scary if you are not walking with obedient faith.

So my thinking goes this way, "What about the part of the body of Christ and the individual that has none of the basic fruit operating in their life? I wonder what then? What will be said to them on that dreadful day?

Will it be said, "Oh, that's ok. It's alright; you can come in fruitless. It was not your fault anyway. It's ok that you buried the seed that I gave you because of fear."

I'm being a little facetious; but you know I am very serious. I'm saying that we see from Scripture some of them were doing the basic works of Christ or at least they thought they were and yet they did not enter in. What of the Christian that shows no works or fruit, what then? Will you take that chance?

There's a solution. If you are a God man, it's better to be obedient to the word of God, walk in step with His Holy Spirit and bear fruit that when it is tried in the fire it will not burn up.

Take up your cross and follow hard after the Lord. This is a life of hope and faith that we are walking out so we must do it trusting in a loving God. And He that has started a good work in us will complete it.

Day 29: Iniquity...

It is very important that you know the word of God, more and more. You should be consistently renewing your mind in the word of God. If you are a born again believer, the Devil would like for you to be ignorant of this revelation.

If there is a sin or a reoccurring problem (situation) that buffets you, always raising its ugly head just when you think it's gone. You may be dealing with an iniquity. Something that has possibly been passed down to you from generations before. And I mean that. It may have gone through several generations without interruption.

I've seen it with males in their promiscuity, adultery and women with a spirit of control beyond description. It's a bad case of the spirit of Jezebel that will keep going from generation to generation, if you allow it.

I say you, because, most likely, no one else in your family has come to this point. The point where you can make a decision to see it change. It will take a big dose of courage to believe God in deliverance, not to mention, the power of the Holy Spirit.

But it must be revealed and dealt with by the Spirit of God. It will help to be in a good church that teaches the word of God in power. Or it (the iniquity) will just keep, going and going and going the generations. Unless, Jesus comes first, the Devil has no plans of stopping. You get my point.

And, yes I saw your deliverance last night. Be that one in your family that will breakthrough that family situation and see God get the glory. We live in an ever increasing kingdom. You've been saying, there must be more. There is more in God. You can believe him for more in your life and your family's life.

Day 30: The Big Fat No

I have come to this summation the importance of using the word, "No" in life. We discussed earlier, about saying it to your children. There's also a place for a big fat NO to ourselves and other people. These are life changing times we live in.

If you don't take up your courage and say the word NO, you may spend a life time trying to correct it. Again, this word has to be applied in raising children. But it's, also, needed in gaining and walking in self-control, living a sanctified life, to certain adventures, even to who you decide to marry or not.

The word, No is a very important word. Here's a biblical example where it needed to be applied and it wasn't. King David had many sons. But two of them were famous for their hair and good looks, named Adonijah and Absalom. Adonijah the Bible says his father never interfered with what he did. Meaning, he was never told, no.

Looking at Absalom's life you can tell by what he did that he was never told, no, either. You may know already, the beginning of this matter was David sinned by taking Bathsheba to his bed. The problem was she was another man's wife. King David tried to hide it for a while, so the Lord sent his man of God to tell him a story revealing his sin.

The man of God said to him, "God said, this will the penalty for your sin. The sword will never leave the house of David and out of your family there will be revolt. This is a result of David not using the word, NO to himself and later to his sons. Absalom tried to take his father's kingdom. It caused him to eventually lose his life. It didn't have to be that way.

There was plenty of provision enough for both of the sons. If they had received more NOs, they might have lived longer. I have noticed in life; we have the power to choose. It's our fault if we allow this signature.

If a parent doesn't give enough NOs to their children when they are young, when the children are older they will become the ruler if not carful. And look what happened to Absalom. With wisdom and balance, keep the NO available.

If you are full and satisfied with the word of God in your life that's good. My prayer is that you are using what you have to help a lost world. I am called to the fatherless, the widows, the desperate, the wounded, the lost and broken, the spiritually empty, the hungry. We go to the highways and byways, the sick and those that don't know what to do.

There's almost not a week that passes by that the Lord sends someone that is believing God for a miracle. We agree in prayer. Then explosions happen! I meet and see these people every day and the Lord's grace continues to be sufficient.

Day 31: Are We Babes In Christ, I

Are you growing in Christ? Not long ago, I began to notice the different stages of growth some of us are in. I saw some growing giant slayers, some teen-agers in the faith, baby Christians and all different kinds of growth stages. You know where I'm going but I have to mention it. I, also, saw some pouty Christians that didn't fit the category they were residing in.

The Lord has his ways to help us know when we need to grow up. The other day, my wife and I were walking in the grocery store. As we were looking through one of the isles, there was a young teenager standing in a corner of the store pouting.

When I first saw him, my heart went out for him. I said to myself, oh his mother must have said no to him. I was like, bless his young heart. Then he turned around and we looked at each other in the face.

He had his thumb in his mouth and to my surprise all my sympathies went out the door for him. I was like, bless his heart, he just needs to grow up. I hope he's getting enough NOs in his life to give him balance.

Lest you think I'm bashing the young folks and the mothers start calling me names, let me tell one on myself, as a son. I'm a father and I'm for our young people. I remember they are our future.

So, I couldn't get on him too hard about the matter. I remember way back in the day, I was a young teenager and immature. I went to the store with my mother, after she got off work. I saw these pair of shoes.

I asked her for some shoes that were called Moon Walkers back then. I wanted them bad. Because, in my mind, I knew when I got them, I was going to be so cool! Well, I asked her to buy them for me. The concept hadn't cross my mind that she didn't have the money.

So, I began to beg for them and cry for them. I wailed the whole while we were there in the store. She would say, "Boy, I told you, I don't have the money." But I kept on crying.

To this day, I'm still embarrassed for the way I acted. I regretted that I put that kind of pressure on my mother that day. I was at the beginning of that crazy (immature) adolescence stage in my life.

We're discussing King David's sons and the fact that they didn't get enough NOs. I discuss the story in my book *The Character of King David*. It was one of the hardest of my books to write but the richest.

As the story goes, King David had a son name Adonijah. The word of God says, he was never told no. He was never asked by his father, "Why do you do this, or why do you do that." In short, his father never interfered with him.

To make a long story short, the youngster said within himself, "Today I will be king instead of my father." So, he gathered up fifty or so men to run before him, to proclaim who he thought he was, the king, the successor of the great King David, but he wasn't.

Day 32: Are We Babes In Christ, II

The youngster, Adonijah, eventually lost his life in treachery against his father's kingdom under his brother King Solomon. My point is, it didn't have to go that way. He could've submitted to the authority in place, matured in his father's kingdom and flourished.

There's a continual call to grow up in Christ, each into our own level. With that said, the reason I mention these stories is because some of us are acting that way in the body of Christ. And it's time to grow up. Spiritually, you are walking around with your thumb in your mouth and pouting to get what you want.

The Spirit of the Lord is saying, that's enough. And if we don't heed the Spirit of the Lord, our Father God has his ways in helping us to grow up. I have experienced it and seen it in action. It's not always pretty. It is best for us to yield to His leading and be obedient in submission to the process.

This is a natural process in life, too, you can see it in nature. I've watched nature all my life from dogs, to birds to cats, all kind of wild life. There's always a price to be paid if that animal doesn't learn how to grow up real fast. Some Deer, as soon as they are born and they hit the ground, they get up running. It's the same with other wild animals. There's a need to grow up fast.

We can watch nature and learn from it. We, as loving fathers and mothers, have to let our children mature and grow up. When we don't, we and they pay the price for it and that's never the right way.

So my suggestion is: If you have found this topic fits you, decide to make the change. Say to yourself, I will grow up today! I will become the mature man or woman of God you have called me to be. With the Lord's help, today, I will become all that God has called me to be, in Jesus name!

Day 33: Horrace Ford Beasley

We would call him Grandpa Ford. The first time I remember seeing him I think I was about four or five years old. My family and I lived in St. Louis, Missouri. We would go to Arkansas and visit my mother's parents, Ford and Elizabeth Beasley. They were beautiful people inside and out.

On one of our first visits, I remember my dad was getting at me about something and my Grandmother was saying, "Don't you whip my baby; leave him alone," she saved me and I didn't get a spanking. First thing, Grandpa taught us to fish, me and my four brothers. I'm pretty sure my sister learned how to fish, too.

The first fish, I remember catching, I ran it all the way into the house still on the fishing line screaming, "Look at my fish!" It was a little catfish. When, we moved back to Arkansas, we would go fishing, almost every weekend. We would fish till noon and then swim until the late evening.

I still remember the lakes that we fished in: Bear Creek Lake, White Hall, Long Lake Dream, Spread Lake, Cow Bow, St Francis Lake and about a half a dozen more.

Then there was hunting. I once saw my Grandpa shoot a bird out of the sky with one shot with a pistol. It was on for me. I've been an avid hunter, ever since.

He taught us how to shoot and handle guns with respect. I really taught myself to shoot with a daisy B-B gun. We had the best hunting dogs in the area, Flipsy and Big Boy. They were very good trackers; they could go in any thick brush and push the rabbit out or tree a squirrel or raccoon.

My Grandfather had an eighty-acre farm. We grew everything; you would not believe how everything grows, so well, in Arkansas; the dirt is awesome. I get excited about dirt because I live in Texas. The dirt, here, is some kind of different but I'm used to it, after thirty years of living in the area.

In Arkansas we grew Okra, Corn, Peas, Sweet potatoes, Iris potatoes, Cucumbers, Tomatoes, Butter beans, Water melons, Carrots and I could go on forever. We grew most of all the plants from seeds. We disked the ground first then prepared the rows then planted the seeds, like corn and okra.

We would chop it to keep the weeds down so that the plants would grow to harvest and be choked out. After all this, we took the vegetables to market.

I'm here to tell you, if you want your children to learn through hard work, have them pick an acre of okra, two to three times a week. With any other work, they will say, "Oh that's no work at all." All kinds of work for the rest of their life will be easy.

My Grandfather loved to sing. He had the church quartet singers come over and practice. As they would sing, the house would shake and the dust would rise as they praised the Lord in unison. The tears would flow.

My whole family was a musical family; out of all my brothers and sister, I believe we played almost every instrument, well, almost. I was a saxophone guy. I wanted to share a little bit of my Grandfather's story. I will end with this cute this story.

Once, we went fishing and my Grandfather allowed me to bring a friend with me. When we went to the lake, Grandpa said to my friend, me and my brothers. You guys, must be very careful because the water is deep. He said, at the edge of the water, the banks are strait down, so don't fall in and pay attention to where you are.

Now, this friend of mine, we were real close and we did everything together or at least to that day. For some reason, he decided to do the opposite of what my Grandfather said and a little worst. I was sitting in one spot fishing; he was sitting in another. My Grandfather went over the hill, a little bit.

My friend began to lose his mind. He starting acting bad. He started screaming at the top of his lungs saying, Help! Help! Help! He splashed in the water saying, Help, I'm drowning! He kept on doing it. I don't remember exactly what my reaction was but I know I looked at him like he was crazy. I would never in a life time tempt my grandpa like that.

Well, my Grandpa came running over the hill saying to himself, "My Lord, the boy has come out to the lake with me and now he's drowning…" As he came over the hill to check on him, my friend stopped all the commotion. He had this crazy look on his face. Grandpa was angry and said to, us all, get in the truck; we went home.

That was one of about one hundred trips that I went fishing with my Grandfather. He said after we went home, I will never take that boy fishing with me again, EVER. And he never did! So, the moral of this story is: Don't act a fool when you are being favored; you may be written off for life and he was.

Day 34: God The Father And Your Destiny

Are you destined for greatness? I ask you to ask yourself that; I don't mean it in a prideful manner. I want you to ask yourself in a way of faith. In the word of God, there are many godly characters of greatness. When they started they didn't look so great. It's a little hard to say but the word of God says, in describing Jesus, he was one not much to behold.

David, the great giant slayer, when he started out he was described as ruddy. His brothers treated him like a runt of the family. Joseph was the younger of his brothers, they despised him for his dreams of greatness, threw him in a pit and then sold him as a slave.

Rahab, a known prostitute, had the faith to hide the spies when the Israelites were scheduled by Joshua to destroy the city. She and her family were spared. She was in the lineage of Jesus. She became the 3x great grandmother of King David himself.

My point is all of these people started out as normal humans but they all were destined for greatness and so are we. We, sometimes, start thinking our Bible and faith ancestors are super humans. With that being said, just because we start out with a questionable beginning does not mean it has to end that way.

In fact, the writer of proverbs says, to end well is better than starting well. The Spirit of the Lord says, "Oh, the plans I have for you, plans to bless you, to prosper you, and for you to have good success." —Jeremiah 29:11

When I think of this topic, I can't help but think of the late Dr. Oral Roberts and his great achievements. The reason I mentioned his name is because Earma and I got to serve him and his lovely wife three of the five times they came to our church.

We served them as Armorbearers. Our duties were to pick them up from the airport and take care of them until they boarded back on the plane to leave after a two to three-day stay.

It was a tough assignment not as hard work. But in taking care of him and the mantle he carried. When we first got him to the hotel, he decided to have dinner early. We asked him if he wanted to go to the main diner of the hotel to eat. He said to us, nicely, no.

He explained, "I have a word of the Lord that I must impart to the church. I don't want to impart it, prematurely." Meaning, he didn't want to talk or communicate with someone and release it before time.

So, we stayed in the room and ate. We were careful not to act star struck with such a great man of God. So, we chuckled to ourselves, when he asked, "Do you know who I am and what I've done?"

We said yes and begin to list off some of his well-known accomplishments, so he could know. We said, "It's the way we were trained as Armorbearers to treat you with respect but not awe struck with the fame of a person."

We didn't say this to him, but God has taught us the purpose of fame. That purpose is for his glory and for what he intends. So, I was always, in my spirit, at attention.

When we got him to church, I had already been instructed by our leadership, not to take him up the steps to the pulpit. He was in his older years and it was at least eight steps to the top.

As you probably know by now, as soon as we got in the sanctuary he said to me, "Varn, take your hand and put it around my belt so I don't fall. And let's go up these steps." There we went; it went perfect.

Dr. Roberts was destined for greatness. If you can recall his story, all of his young life he struggled with sickness. As a teenager, in his sickness, he was at death's door but God's grace came and healed him.

This man came from poverty and sickness to raising up the great university ORU University, hospital and all the other great organizations and ministries that flow from that. He became world renowned, becoming the epitome of the word greatness in the Christian world in his generation. In the duty of serving, this great man of God, I have many stories.

One of those times he looked at me and said, "Varn, the Lord is going to bless you and Earma for taking such good of care of me." I looked at him and smiled and said thank you, Dr. Roberts. He smiled and left to get on the plane.

The very next morning, my wife and I were awakened by the Spirit of the Lord. We both got up, looked at each other and began to prophesy, all morning. We haven't stopped since. To God be the glory! Thank you, Dr. Oral Roberts, we love you!

Day 35: Next Generation Giant slayers, I

Years ago, the Lord allowed my father and me to have a relationship before he went to be with the Lord. In that season of my life I was just starting to preach and my father saw it in me.

Between him and my Uncle, Rev. Spencer Brown, they allowed me to start my preaching ministry in their pulpits. My father ordained me as a Baptist minister. I am very thankful. Quite a few people ask me, "Aren't you a non-denominational minister?" My answer is always yes, but I'm first a Christian believer. Which simply means, I cross the denominational lines.

Anyway, my wife and I were living in Dallas, in that time of my life, we were busy in the jail and prison ministry and just started becoming Armorbearers. We were busy every weekend teaching on Saturday mornings and preaching on Sunday evenings. Whenever we got the chance to go to Arkansas it was a sacrifice, but we went.

When we went, we were always prepared to preach, between my uncle's two churches and my father's two churches. I always had a place to preach and practice my skills when I went home. On one of those Sundays, at my father's church, the Lord spoke to me in my heart these words. "Saul has killed his thousands and David his tens of thousands."

Surprisingly, I knew exactly what the Spirit of the Lord was saying. I knew that he was talking about my father and me; I was listening. The time that the Lord allowed me to spend with my father was important. I believe that an assignment was transferred. As a little kid, I always knew that my father loved the Lord. I could see it, even as a child.

I saw his struggles and his passion for the Lord. He fell down but he kept getting up and re-signing up as a minister of God. One of the things, I really admired is when he sang before preaching. He was very good at them both. He must have passed that on to me because I love to sing and preach. I believe I'm pretty good.

The Sunday the Lord spoke that word to me I knew the Lord was speaking about the assignment that was given to my father and now to me. In John 14:12, "Very truly I tell you, whoever believes in me will do the works I have been doing, and they will do even greater things than these, because I am going to the Father." These words our Lord has spoken are the reason I'm in expectancy and believing God for even greater works.

Remember, we serve our Lord in an ever increasing kingdom of God. We should increase in every generation. And it should not be a prideful thing. Don't get me wrong, I'm not comparing my father to Saul.

But you do remember the story where Saul fell short because of disobedience. He was not able to fulfill the complete assignment that was given of the Lord because of his disobedience and rebellion. Because of that he left this life prematurely.

I'm sad to say, I know this happens more than not. David was chosen of the Lord to fulfill the call. He had a time receiving the mantle. Saul made sure David wouldn't walk straight into it while he was living. Because Saul had lost his mantle, he didn't want anyone else to have it. But the fact remains, David did receive it. He went on to become one of the greatest kings that ever lived besides the King of kings.

Day 36: Next Generation Giant Slayers, II

Saul was in a very hard place. The Prophet Samuel had died and he was receiving no word from the Lord. Saul thought within himself and said, "Since the Lord won't speak to me, I will find a Seer." And that's what he did. He disguised himself because he had banned all Seers in the land, knowing it's against God's law to seek the occult.

When the Seer saw that he was Saul, she screamed for dear life and made Saul swear to her that he wouldn't kill her; so he swore. Saul asked the Seer to bring up Samuel the prophet from the grave to help him; for he was in dire circumstances. Since, he could hear no word of the Lord, the seer conjured up Samuel.

The Bible says, Samuel said, "Why have you disturbed me?" Saul answered because the Lord has forsaken me and he will not answer me; so I asked that you be brought up to help me. Samuel said to him in his spirit form, tomorrow you and your sons will be joining me in death; Saul waxed faint and would not eat. Saul's servants repeatedly begged him to eat but he would not... —I Samuel 28: 3-25

So, when I speak of this I'm not comparing my father's sins to Saul, because all our sin is as hideous, before the Lord. That's why we are so thankful for the blood of Jesus. This story does let us know that we can cancel our assignment of the Lord, if we tend to have a stint toward sin without repenting.

My father had problems before the Lord; only the Lord knows if that's why he left this earth, prematurely. I do know his problems with alcohol didn't help and caused him to fall short. So, in God's grace, he accomplished what he could in his life time. And the same with your parents. Now it's our turn. That's where we come in.

The giants are still there and their family members like Goliath. They have to be slain; meaning we can't let that enemy win; we must defeat them so they can't fight the next generation.

I heard someone say, that's why David had five smooth stones when he slew Goliath. One was for Goliath and the others were for his brothers. David was the warrior, so am I and so are you in your generation. As for me and my family, I am well up for the task.

So, in the saying, "Saul has killed his thousands and David his tens of thousands." I did see the work of God that my father did and I honor him. But I do recognize the Lord has called me much further saying it respectfully. The Lord has shown me one hundred acres full of people ready for harvest. And I'm about my father's business, slaying giants as I go! What about you?

Day 37: The Prodigal Prince

I saw a friend a little while ago, he is a son of old friends of mine. When I first met him, he was a young boy. He is his father's son. He is a prince. Although I met him a few times, I personally don't know him very well. I am in distant relationship with his parents.

Anyway, when I saw him, the first thing I thought to myself was, "Man, he looks just like his father."

Then I said looking at him, "He is his father's namesake." The reason I'm writing this is, my heart goes out to him and others like him.

From the circumstances, I see, I wonder if he's making decisions without his father's counsel. Still looking at him, standing up there looking just like him (his father), same face, same stance.

I begin to think, if I could make a law in the Laws of God this would be two of them. The first would be that you have to have God in your life as Lord and Savior. The second would be, you shouldn't make a life changing decision without a father's consent or approval.

Now, I must say here, I am not speaking of any of my family members, thank the Lord. I say this with grace, because I could be, just as easily be in the same situation. It could happen to anybody. Anyone of us could make a wrong choice and our life would be different, right?

Now back to the prince. Even though, sometimes we go on and do our own thing, you are still under God's grace. Remember, there is God's perfect will and God's permissive will. And there may be some consequences to walk through. Even so, after our mistakes, God will work it to our good. He promised.

Speaking of the prince and people like him, I could look straight in his face and know and he knows where he's standing. The sure thing about it is, time will always tell. If your plan that you made works, then all is well, but if it doesn't, all will tell.

You see that is why God has devised it that we need a father's help. And we should take advantage of it, especially if he has given us a good father. Which in the prince's case, God has given him a good father.

No one's perfect; but judging his fruit, I can tell. I could go on but I will stop here; I will say this: Even, if you have made the worst decision in your life, that doesn't mean your intentions were not good when you did it. We're human; sometimes we miss it.

Or maybe the reason you made the bad decision is because you are still mad at your father for whatever reason. Remember this. There is still your father's love and you can run to it.

I'm praying for you, the prince and all of the prodigals. I don't say that in a bad way because I was once a prodigal. I did just what I'm about to tell you to do.

Repent and run to your father's arms! Prince, your position is vacant and it needs to be filled by you, alone. God has kingdom purpose for you. He won't settle for anything less. And neither should you.

Day 38: Receive Ye Spiritual Fathers

The writer of I Corinthians 4:15 said, "For though ye have ten thousand instructors in Christ, yet have ye not many fathers, for in Christ Jesus I have begotten you through the gospel."

Paul the Apostle is instructing the Church on its need for spiritual fathers and says to them, there is a need for many. He says to them, "You have many instructors in Christ but there is still a need." We have singing instructors, dancing, speaking, studying, tutoring, praying, writing, reading, golfing, football, baseball, basketball and the list could go on.

I believe we get the point, he says, "Though ye have ten thousand instructors in Christ yet ye have not many fathers." We can only be instructed so far then there is a need of fathers and a need for many.

As a father there is a bigger investment in the deal. You being their son or daughter, you will not be able to get away with things that aren't good for you. They will make sure you stay on the right track.

There's not a lack of spiritual fathers in the church. There's not a lack of men and women that are willing to be used by the Holy Spirit as a "spiritual father" that covers. The spiritual father covers you, cares for you, loves you, nurtures you, reproves you and yes even rebukes you.

He supports you in your baseball games, studies home-work with you, cries with you, and prays with you. The Apostle Paul says, "Ye have a need of many fathers." He has the authority to say to the Church, I have begotten you so take heed to my saying, "Receive ye many fathers!"

They are all around you. Perhaps, he was that teacher that you thought was so hard on you. Or that Uncle or Aunt that never let up on you until you did what was right.

You thought they were the meanest person around but they were acting by the Holy Spirit giving you what you needed, even fathering you when you needed it most.

So, if you feel that you are fatherless, you don't have to be. God has commanded his Church in saying, "Receive ye spiritual fathers!" Look around and receive your father.

Day 39: Pruned If You Do And Pruned If You Don't

Do you know why our God is called Father God? It's because he fathers us! We have all had fathers that did their best to give us the best for ourselves. So, how much more will our heavenly Father know what to do for us? God's gives us loving chastisement.

Do you know that by you being a child of God, He will not allow you to get away with what others get away with? And the reason for that is, you are His sons and daughters.

When we go through valleys in our life. We must make sure that we learn our lessons that our heavenly Father is trying to teach us. Especially when you've prayed a fox hole prayer. Be sure to honor God with what you have said, less you find yourself back there again, and its worst. Obey Him and live a great life.

When I was young, my mother would take a belt to me, whenever I got out of line. And I can say, most of the time, I knew I deserved it.

Single Moms & The Fathering Spirit

Here's a quick story about the fathering spirit that worked through my Mom. I know a lot of you single moms will relate to this. My precious mother raised us six kids as a single mom, having to be both parents in one.

She had the support of our grandparents and other male relatives in the community. But for the most part, the buck stopped with her being a mother and father to us.

So, anyway, she told me not to go uptown and play ball, she didn't want me getting in trouble. I ended up going anyway, deciding to do my own thing. The ball game, I went and played in, my arm got broken.

It didn't get set until twelve o'clock that night. I never forgot it. It was a lesson learned about disobeying a direct order from my mother. My mother was a fun Mom; she didn't keep a tight rein on us. (Probably couldn't – worked all the time) When she did lay the law down, she meant it.

Now, I know you're probably saying, I read those Scriptures earlier. All I can say is, somethings are just worth repeating. Now, go ahead read them again.

For whom the Lord loves He chastens, And scourges every son whom He receives. If you endure chastening, God deals with you as with sons; for what son is there whom a father does not chasten? But if you are without chastening, of which all have become partakers, then you are illegitimate and not sons.

Furthermore, we have had human fathers who corrected us, and we paid them respect. Shall we not much more readily be in subjection to the Father of spirits and live? For they indeed for a few days chastened us as seemed best to them, but He for our profit, that we may be partakers of His holiness.

Now no chastening seems to be joyful for the present, but painful; nevertheless, afterward it yields the peaceable fruit of righteousness to those who have been trained by it. —Hebrews 12:6-11

Pruned If You Do And Pruned If You Don't

My advice is to stop trying to save your brothers and sisters when the Lord is doing his work. Less you get in on it! I remember my mother saying, "Boy move your hands!"

Either way, whatever you do won't save you from God's correction. Remember, we were born into sin, so we all need correction at some point in our lives. And that's why I agree with the quote, "Pruned if you do and pruned if you don't."

With all that said, obedience does make us eligible for the blessings that only the obedient can receive. So, its best children of God, be an obedient child of God.

Day 40: Are You Hindered By Insecurities

Are you trying to trust God yet feeling insecure at the same time? What a lot of people don't know about that word is, it can change you into another person, if you're not healed from it. That spirit of, 'you're not God enough' will lie to you so much, you will think it's your own voice.

And remember, whether you know it or not, it can start at the beginning of your life, when you are very young. It can happen so young and so quick, you will take it on as yourself, and think it's normal. Most times, it starts with some trauma, some hurtful event that was never addressed in your life and many times indirectly or directly related to your father or the absence of his presence to protect you. But, let's look at some defining words then the word of God first.

Insecure: (Of a person) not confident or assured; uncertain and anxious. Synonyms: unconfident, uncertain, unsure, doubtful, hesitant, self-conscious, unassertive, diffident, unforthcoming, shy, timid, retiring, timorous, inhibited, introverted. I must say, if two or three of these are active in your life. You may be, insecure. I have to say this, if you have dealt with being fatherless a lot of these symptoms seem to naturally come with it.

Years ago I was working for a boss. I had only been working for him for about a year or so. I was new at a lot of things that I was supposed to do. So I may have made a few mistakes. To make a long story short, I was given the master keys to the property so that I could help assist my boss better.

But I made a mistake and went in another manager's office to get keys to a rental car for a guest worker. The car keys were supposed to be left accessible to me.

When the other manager came in, he was upset about me going into his office. We got into it verbally. From my perspective, we were about to fight, well I was.

When my boss came in he looked at me and said, "Varn, what's going on? I told him about the situation. I felt I had merit. In a slightly heated conversation, I said to him, if the manager had pushed me verbally one more time, I would have punched him.

When I said that, at that moment, I knew I had said the wrong thing. My boss looked at me and said, in a nice but sad voice, "Varn, you're just insecure."

And my ignorant response was, "I may be, but I was about to smack him."

Well you can guess, it became a learning season for me, my boss made sure of it. To tell the truth, I'm still on that journey, learning and working this one out. You see I was wading in an ocean of insecurities and didn't know it.

You see my personality is that of a nonviolent person. I have been in only one fight in my life and I was defending myself then.

But if you are insecure, almost any situation can be created in yourself and you really don't have any merit with insecurity. Most times, you're just fighting because you think you have been wronged. When I mention these scenarios, I'm not just talking about myself to be talking about myself. I'm always hoping someone will see themselves in what I'm saying and do what I did, turn to God for help.

So, really you're mad because of past hurts you have received that are unhealed and covered up. Many times, we don't even remember what started us to feeling insecure.

Surprising to me, I had never considered the possibility, about me being insecure. So a journey of seeking information and healing began. I was familiar with the word, but I had not considered it about myself.

Day 41: Father God And The Generations, I

How do you think the God of Abraham deals with a rebellious people, when they have a heart after foreign gods? I want to tell you a story about how the God of Abraham dealt with a nation that had gone to Idol worship. They had forsaken their living God for a God of substance, does that sound familiar?

This is where it all began. There was a righteous king that loved his God with all his heart. His love was so strong and faithful; he would set the bar on how we should worship. So much so, it's still set to this day. He loved his God so much; he danced before him with all his might.

When the time came for him to be with his forefathers, he had a son ready to pick it up where he left off as King. He would charge him to do right before the Lord. He said to his son, 'If you will love the Lord your God, he will keep you and protect you and make you prosper. But if you change your mind and follow foreign gods, he will forsake you and cast you out.

His son became a reward to him and became the wisest man on the face of the earth. His life proved it, to a certain point. There's only a few things this King would do bad, even though he was the wisest man on the face of the earth. He had a heart problem. He gave it to all his foreign wives instead of his God.

They turned his heart to do the things that his father warned him not to do, like worshipping foreign gods. God appeared to him twice. He said of him in his latter life of disobedience, "Since you have decided to be this way about serving me; this is what I will do. I will give your kingdom to another man."

God's Great Mercy

But out of God's great mercy he said, "I won't do it in your generation but in the next one, your son's generation." This is where it began, with God dealing with a rebellious nation of people. He does it by giving them what they wanted, through their own chosen leadership. You see, they chose their king.

By now, this was the third generation from the man of God that danced before the Lord with all his heart. He did it so well, God said there would be no one like him. Well this is his grandson's chance to get it right.

I'm a little ahead of myself; so let me back up a little bit. The son of the great man of God had a problem. When you don't do what you're supposed to do you are replaced. And here is his replacement. Now pay attention to this guy, because for sure you will be familiar with him, even for today.

There was a man of God and the word of God came to him and said, "I have chosen the next king for my people Israel. This is what I want you to do. Take a coat and tear it into twelve pieces. Give it to this man I have chosen. Give him ten of them and the other two will stay with the king of Judah.

When the man of God saw him he gave him the word of the Lord and the ten pieces of cloth. And said to him, "You shall be King of the Israelites."

You see, God had planned it this way so that he might punish them for their idol worship and rebellion. God decided to punish them through, their leadership, and he did. Afterwards, the man had to flee to Egypt because the king that lost ten of his tribes tried to kill him.

Don't forget, it was in all God's plan. Eventually the king died and the one that received the word of the Lord and the ten pieces returned. The ten pieces stood for the ten tribes of Israel.

As soon as the new fella, the new king received his ten tribes of Israel he said to himself, out of fear, "I must change all the rules and not allow my people to go and worship in Israel. Because if I do, they will kill me and go back to their old king. So this is what I will do.

About the same time, he received counsel and decided to do the worst of all kings, he made altars and two golden calves. He placed one altar in Bethel and the other all the way in Dan. The people went even that far to worship.

This was a great sin before the eyes of the Lord. Yet, it was the Lord's intent so that he might punish the Israelites. The unwise king went even as far as to have man ordained festivals. Even worst, he made priest out of whoever he wanted to become one.

The Word Of The Lord

The word of the Lord came to the man of God and the Lord said, "Go to the altar."

So, one day as the king was having one of his ceremonies, the man of God came and spoke to the altar and said, "There shall be a son named Josiah that will be born to the house of David that shall sacrifice these priest on this altar. And human bones will be burned on you. And this shall be the sign, the altar will be split into and the ashes will spill on the ground."

At that moment, the altar split and the ashes spilled on the ground. When the king saw this he pointed his hand at the man of God and said, "Seize him!"

And when he did, his hand shriveled up and he screamed, "Man of God intercede for me!"

The man of God interceded for the king and his hand was restored as before. The king said to him, "Can I give you a gift? Will you come home and eat with me?"

He said to him, "I cannot receive a gift from you. I was commanded not to eat, drink or return from the way I came but to leave in one direction" So he left.

Now I know you may be saying, "Varn what in the heck does all that have to do with me?"

I would have to say, do you know that we serve that same God. Even though we have the grace of the Cross; He is the same God. The God of Abraham, Isaac, and Jacob. He's the same yesterday, today and forever. Also, He's a jealous God and has commanded, we shall have no other Gods before us.

In our generation we make gods out of cars, houses, games, money, things, and other people. Yet He said, "You shall have none before me."

Day 42: Father God And The Generations, II

God often deals with us through our leadership. You see, in the case of Israel, he used the nation's leadership to deal with the people. I believe this speaks for the same situation, we're in today. I'm not pointing the finger at anyone specific, any authorities because they have all had their issues, from White Water, young aides like Ms. Lewinsky, to the Gulf War. Even, at the time of this writing, the current President who's still trying to prove he's a Christian President amidst his liberal stance. Yes, there are liberal Christians.

Yet, we are a nation that wants to put the blame on someone. God uses trouble to deal with his people, us, and even (Humanity) at large. He uses it to drive a weary soul home.

Remember, that was his intent. Oh yes, the king I've been describing to you was named Jeroboam! And his title created from his sinful life echoes through the generations, "The Sins of Jeroboam!"

Because of his sin before God, he was given over to it (himself – his own desires.) It always surprises me that the Lord will allow us to revile in our sin for a season, (lifetime) then he was called on it. Remember the Apostle Peter said, we should not consider it that God is letting people get away with their sin. Yet, it is His great Mercy and Longsuffering that no one might perish but come to their senses and repentance. — 2 Peter 3:9

Jeroboam fate was, he died in it. His son became sick; so he told his wife to go and see the Prophet Ahijah. He had her disguise herself and take the man of God a gift and ask him if their son would live.

The Lord told the prophet that she was coming. Then he told him what to say. He said to her when she came, "As soon as you step over the doorstep of your home, 'Your son will die."

The prophet words from God came to pass, he did die just when he said he would.

Jeroboam would eventually die in his sin but the bigger tragedy was that he left a wicked legacy. He led a nation into great sin and they all paid for it. Jeroboam passed his sin on to another generation, his son, and the Lord used it to deal with his people Israel.

The Death of His Son

Nadab, son of Jeroboam, became king of Israel. He also, did evil in the eyes of the Lord, walking in the ways of his father and in his sin which he had caused Israel to commit. Baasha killed Nadah in the third year of Asa king of Judah and succeeded him as king.

As soon as he began to reign, he killed Jeroboam's whole family. He did not leave Jeroboam anyone that breathed but destroyed them all, according to the word of the Lord given through his servant Ahijah the Shilonite, because of the sins Jeroboam had committed and had caused Israel to commit, and because he provoked the Lord, the God of Israel to anger. —I Kings 15:25-30

All Authority Given From God

I have been taught in my Christian walk before the Lord, that the Lord gives us the authority that's over us. In his sovereignty, the authority that's given, is what we should have.

Jacob, before he wrestled with God, his name was translated, grabber. The story goes, 'as his brother was being born before him,' he grabbed his leg. Jacob's authority was his uncle and he gave him hell; he made him work fifteen years to marry his daughter. Can you see it yet? God sent him that authority to help him deal with himself.

There are many examples in the word of God. We should know that the Lord still does the same thing, even in this time. If we as a nation would humble ourselves and present a righteous heart before Lord, He would hear our prayers and send us a righteous king, (president).

The word of God says all Scripture is God-breathed and is useful for teaching, rebuking, correcting and training in righteousness – 2 Timothy 3:16 I felt led by the Holy Spirit to teach this now.

So, won't you join me in taking this as a lesson and learn from the disobedience of Jeroboam and the Israelites. We have to repent and make sure we're not making the same mistakes in idolism and worshiping foreign gods.

In God's great mercy and longsuffering, there's a reason we are called the most blessed of all nations. May we all do our very best to walk worthy through Christ of such a great honor to be in such a nation.

Excerpt from book: The Character of King David.

Day 43: The Beggar At The Door, I

A few years ago, I was asked by a pastor friend of mine to offer my services as an arborist on a U. S. mission trip to help restore a church. This friend of mine, I have big respect for; so I said yes before he could finish asking me the question.

Even so, this trip meant missing work and sowing a week's worth of work into the mission. It was a big deal and a sacrifice for us. Yet, my wife and I both agreed we could do it and counted it as an opportunity for the glory of God and the Kingdom.

The first thing I did was Google the property online and took a look at the trees, so I would know what tools to take with me. I said to myself, "Oh, they're just thirty to forty feet tall. It will be a walk in the park for me to trim them.

One thing I wasn't able to prepare for online was the elevation; it was six thousand feet above sea level. I got there and saw the trees were not exactly as they appeared online. They were twice as tall, I immediately knew, man I've got my work cut out.

It was hard for me to breathe for a couple of days but I survived. At the time of this writing, I had trimmed trees for almost thirty years, after adjusting it became just another job for me. Don't get me wrong it was a lot of work involved. It took me several days; but I got it done.

On our way back home, I was so excited that I had accomplished the task that was sat before me. I was very excited to be going home to see my wife. This mission and the church was birthed for a people that couldn't pay us back. My pastor friend and his family birthed it out of a compassionate heart toward this people.

So again, the Lord blessed me to complete my task. I finished it in about three and a half days. I was tired but I finished. So on the way back, we had eleven hundred miles to go driving and I was trying to be patient.

We stopped at a McDonalds to get breakfast and I was the first to go inside. On the way up to the door, there was a Native Indian lying by the door in a drunken stupor, like the beggar at the gate, asking for anything I could give him. I looked at him with compassion and said, "I'm all out of money."

You see when I took the trip, I was in a slow season of my business and I was only able to take a one-hundred-dollar bill and the week there had already taken it. So, he looked at me as if I hadn't said anything. If you know me, it's very hard for me to pass anybody that's in need.

Remember, my wife and I led a team to feed the homeless at our local church for years. So, I said to the homeless Indian, "You see that van of men over there? They are all godly men. Go over and knock on the van door and ask them for some money. They will be glad to get you something to eat." I pointed the vehicle out to him and went inside.

It did not go the way I thought it would go. Now, I don't want you to think that we got into it but you can be for sure, we had a serious debate. I must admit, I'm not always the debating kind.

As soon, as I opened the door they said, "VARN!!!" Did you send that drunk man over here to ask us for money? It was about three to four people with similar questions, at the same time. It went like this. Why did you send that man? We thought he was about to rob us or something. Multiply the questions about three times and that's what happened. They were half laughing and half serious.

Then came the debating, I was in no mood for debating and there is a reason. For me debating had always led to something worst, so I don't do it much. But we did.

You see, I was at the bottom of the authority chain in this group. I was ok with that. I, always, do my best to gird myself in respect. I know that I'm always planting seed for my future in authority. But, that's another topic for another time!

Back to the story. We debated; almost every leader drilled me in asking why I felt led to help that homeless drunk man. Questions were thrown at me, like, did you help him because you wanted to fulfill your religious convictions? Don't you know it enables a person when you help them? Maybe you helped because you feel by doing it, you will make your way into heaven or something like that?

Or you helped him because you see other people doing it and you want the notoriety? It went on for a while; it seemed like about thirty minutes. You should know It wasn't mean-spirited but I was being drilled and my motives being questioned. I'm a big guy so I could take it.

Day 44: The Beggar At The Door, II

Now truthfully, I hadn't thought about the answer behind my actions. But that situation forced me to come to a conclusion. I thought about our earlier ministry, I mentioned to you earlier in the earlier devotional. We led a small group of about thirty to fifty people in our church where we fed the homeless under the bridges of downtown Dallas for years.

So, I was used to helping the poor. We gave out two hundred or more bags of food and two truckloads of clothes every month. But that's not a reason, I could offer them.

Out of the pressure, my answer came. It was as unexpected to me as it was to my brothers in Christ. It came with tears. It was about seven or more of us, a van full of men, all men's kind of men. I told them a story about myself and my dad.

There's a long version in my book *'Healing the Wounds of a Fatherless Generation'* but I gave them the short version. If you're interested in the full story, visit me at http://varnbrown.com and send for your copy or order a bundle for your men's ministry group to read through.

Back to the story, I said in the city I grew up in, my father was one of the town drunks. He was one of the bums that walked around the city drunk, asking people for money or food. As a young teenager, a few times, I would be walking with my friends and see him and feel ashamed.

In tears I said, I guess when I see a person down in life, I think it's like my father was. If I could just give them something to help them hold on until their help — their deliverance comes...

I went on with my story: One time I went home to Arkansas to visit. As I was driving around, I saw my Dad lying on his back, drunk in the middle of a ditch. It was a beautiful day; I was feeling good. I was driving a nice car but when I saw him, my heart sank.

I pulled over on the side of the road and got out to talk to him. He got up as soon as he saw me. You can imagine what I saw as he struggled to stand up.

As soon as he got up out of the ditch, I began to weep and I couldn't stop. My father said to me, "Son, why are you crying?"

I said, "I don't know. I guess it's the Holy Spirit." After a while, he got into my car. I took him home. There's a good ending to this part of this story.

Until his death, I never saw him drunk again. You see, he was a struggling minister. I can even say God raised my Daddy out of the ditch.

After he was back on his feet, he started pastoring again. As I've been telling you in this book, that's why it was such a big deal that I was honored to preach several of his church anniversaries before his passing.

After I told them that story, I began to weep and maybe them too. At any rate, the debating ceased.

Other than that, I had a blast! It was one of the best mission trips I've ever taken.

Day 45: The Job Factor

Have you experienced suffering, trouble, setbacks or reversals? Get ready. I have some fatherly advice coming at you. In the life of Job, there was evidence of his righteousness to the point that God bragged on him to Lucifer.

God said to him, "Have you seen my servant Job?" Lucifer said, "Yes I've seen him." He is blessed."

Yet, if you take the hedge of protection down from around him and let me attack him, he will curse you." If you read the story you know how it went.

The point I want to make is, in God's kingdom there are different reasons for suffering. The Job factor is one of them. If you're a faithful Christian and you've been experiencing some suffering, God may have been bragging on you too.

So, there is Job-like suffering, the prophets who suffer, the godly that suffer; we share in Christ's suffering so we share in His glory. If He suffered, we're no greater than Him, right?

All suffering is not because of sin. In Job's case, it was so Father God could prove a point. I like to say God made a bet and won. I like saying that, but I'm not a gambling man.

We, as Christians, must be very careful when we want to make a judgment call against someone because they are going through a tough trial.

The reason I say this is, look at what happened to the friends of Job. Most of the chapter of Job are his friends explaining how they knew he sinned. Why else would he be going through such troubles, they asked?

They were wrong and almost died because of it. God said to them, "Go have Job pray for you so that I may hear his prayer and forgive you, that you may be restored." —Job 42:5-10

We as the body of Christ must have an understanding that we are on the same team. When we fight one another and speak against one another the enemy gets the upper hand and we fall short.

When we speak against one another as brothers and sisters, God chastises us to get us back in line.

The best thing to do when we see someone in the middle of a battle or a raging storm is to pray for them.

For the storms of life will come to us all and we would be smart not to create our own.

No matter what you are going through sunny days or stormy, the grace of Father God is always sufficient!

Day 46: My Fruit And Your Fruit

I was thinking and talking to a friend. What if we could calculate all of the souls that the Lord used us to lead to him, by the power of the Lord? Now, I don't want to stop there; I want to go farther.

Imagine, the person that you led to the Lord. Then imagine the persons that they led to the Lord, and so on. It keeps going and going. It never stops. Have you been one of those type of Christians that would count the souls that you led to the Lord?

Now, I'm not saying that anything is wrong with that. It's the way it is sometimes. But at some point, you just stop counting. Well I personally passed that point many years ago.

The reason I wrote this is so that, you would know me and hopefully see yourself. The word of God says, know them that dwell among you. So there you go, that's my story!

My hope is that you see yourself answering the ministry call of God in your life. My prayer is that you see yourself growing and walking in your destiny just like Earma and I are doing. For those who this is for, follow us as we follow Christ. May my story spur you to the good works that God has called you to do.

A Father's Blessing

My father ordained me before he passed at the early age of 64. He battled alcoholism for most of his life. I believe, for the most part, it was the cause of his early demise. One of the last services that the Lord allowed me to preach for him was his church anniversary.

Yes, I know I've spoken to you many times by now. I bring it up again for the ones that haven't even heard it once and the ones that have heard it, I have something more to say that's important. So, bear with me.

The Spirit of the Lord spoke to me about the whole ordeal, about him (my dad) loving the Lord and falling short in certain areas of his life and leaving this earth too soon. He pointed out with what he was given he did his best. Even about the Lord's grace allowing me to be raised up for such a time as this.

The Spirit of the Lord said to me that day, "Saul has slain his thousands and David his tens of thousands." I knew immediately what the Lord was saying. Dad did the best with what he could do; now it's my time. And now it's your time. I'm still on that journey. This mandate is for an almost lost generation that's calling out my name in prayer. I'm answering that call daily.

Day 47: God The Father

I was thinking about the Spirit of the Father, speaking of Father God. His love that he has for us, and how he keeps us covered. You know our story, my father did his best with what he was given. My grandfather was God's backup plan for my life and my family's life.

The grace of God made sure I was ready before Grandpa went to glory. For my life now, the Lord has filled my life with spiritual fathers, and the Lord has been very faithful to me. Now, I look over my life and I can truly say that the Lord has never forsaken me, nor left me fatherless.

The beautiful thing about it now is, I am the father now and have spiritually fathered many already. I know it's the Lord's will that I father many more by the spirit, for the kingdom sake.

Trimming Our Candlesticks

Sometimes it falls on us as Christians to discuss a matter so that it may be dealt with. But we should be quiet about certain things, and be careful about what format we are speaking from.

This is one of those topics, so I'm being careful. The word of God says, once a Devil has been cast out it will return after a season, seeing the house has been swept clean. It returns and brings seven more devils, and the state of the person will be worst then at first.

I have read this scripture many times but have never seen it in action before. I see a season of the enemy's tactics and they are doing their checking. They are checking on houses that are swept clean and abandoned.

Not being kept, filled with the Spirit of God they become accessible again. We as Christian must make sure that our candlewicks are trimmed and our vessels are full of oil. Because the enemy is doing his inspection and seeing who he can convince to go in his direction. So Saints stay the course.

Put Your Hands To The Plow And Don't Pull Back

Are you a shirker of your task? Do you remember the story about the man that was given the talent and out of fear he buried it? Matthew 25:15 He did not have the same spirit as the other men that was given talents. I believe you can use this word in this case as money or gifting.

Well in this case the other man (woman), they took the talent and brought back more, some brought back five, some two and some according to the gift they were given.

But the first character buried his talent in fear, saying to himself. My Lord I know that you are a hard task master, so out of fear I hid it and put it in a hole. So no one else could find it, so that when you asked for it again I could produce it and give it back to you.

And I myself would be ok, with receiving your judgment. Now that sounds selfish doesn't it? He buried it so that he himself would make it through, not thinking of anyone else. He didn't know his master was giving the talent as a test, and he failed it badly.

I was thinking yesterday and it came to me. Do you know that when you are given an assignment from an authority that's in your life, it is similar as when you were given your talent?

We are judged by the same balancer. When you are given a task do you hide and only work when your master (Leader) is looking, or do you not work as hard when you know he's not looking.

When I say master, you know I'm talking about Jesus, right! We must be careful because God is always looking and he is the author of giving out the blessings and promotions. —Ephesians 6:7

Day 48: Seven Things Grandpa Taught Me Our Kids Should Know, I

This is a story about my young life, the pleasurable moments and valuable lessons I learned growing up in Arkansas with my grandparents next door, taking up the slack for my Mom, a single mother with six kids.

These are from the beginning days when our family arrived there from St. Louis Missouri. My family and I stayed with my grandfather for a good season until my mother had our house built. My grandfather and uncle built the house.

Whenever I hear about or speak of carpentry, it makes me think of this. What's not surprising to me about the whole thing is, Earma my wife and I knew of each other in high school. We never got a chance to say anything to each other and I'm glad.

I always tell her; I wasn't ready; I was too immature. Anyway, we grew up in the same Arkansan area and eventually, met and married in Dallas. We call it God's destiny. Now about those lessons I learned from Grandpa that our children should know about.

1. **Learning The Power Of A Trade:** I love carpentry.
    We (Earma and I) both figured out that my grandfather and uncle built their house, too. I actually knew it when I first went into their family's house. Because it is a similar track home to my mother's house. Back to my story, some of my first jobs that I learned to do were in carpentry. I became a professional carpenter but first I was a professional nail straightener. You see back in the day, there wasn't a very large supply of nails because of cost, I'm sure. Every nail that wasn't being used, I would use it. If it was bent, I would straighten it out and nail something with it.

I remember helping my grandfather put the wooden floors down. In that day, they didn't have plywood; they used 1x4x8 boards and we nailed them down. They still use the same technique now in wooden floors. I learned my carpentry skills from helping my Grandfather.

I was always making benches and tables in the backyard with bent nails (straightened out of course by, yours truly) He enjoyed seeing me do it. Because of him, I became a very skilled carpenter, especially in framing with two 28 oz. hammers on my belt, sinking a 16 penny nail in three hits all day long.

Back in those days, there were no air guns. I remember when we started using them. I have helped build many houses and apartments. I specialized in putting on roofs and three story apartments.

I worked only carpentry for about a decade. Here's a quick story: I was on a carpentry job working for a man with about twenty guys. It was right around the corner from my church, Agape Church in Little Rock, Arkansas, years ago.

We were all framing the second floor walls. Can you see it, a bunch of sweaty men, dusty with saw dust all over us, in shorts spitting and chewing tobacco, making a bunch of noise?

As men, they were saying Lord knows what. For some reason, I was the one that a few of the men thought to boss around, with a bit of persecution within it.

I was probably deemed the good Christian. It had gone on for a few weeks. I was a new Christian and on fire in Jesus. In those days, I wouldn't let anyone curse around me or I would call them on it

Well, that day we were on the second floor and a storm came up real fast. The boss was thinking we should consider stopping and going down, but we hadn't. So, we kept working.

Like they would say in the old days. "This is the God's truth." A large, black cloud came over us. Right before we could move, I heard a voice say to me, "If the lightning strikes, will you get struck by lightning?

And I said, "No, because I'm covered by the blood of Jesus." Suddenly, a boom, sounded off like a major explosion had gone off about fifty feet above our heads.

Some of the men jumped to their feet, we all hollered. A few seconds later, I began to tell them what I heard. They just looked at me. The main persecutor that was giving me so much trouble was on his knees, rubbing his arm back and forth because the electricity amperage had gone through the cord and temporally paralyzed his arm; it was all red.

I didn't get any more persecution from that day forth. Funny thing, for years I was thinking that mostly about the Devil trying to kill me. And that may have been true. That was in the late Eighties. But it came to me a few months ago, now that I walk in this mantle, that's upon my life. It's more about God making a distinction. A few of the men were saved.

Encourage your children to learn a trade and not just get an education, especially the ones that are more hands on. Don't get me wrong, I'm not saying an education is not important.

After all the years, the opportunity was not there and all the years of drilling into our children to get an education, I can't say that. But I do say learning a trade is a good thing.

Let your children work with you; there may be one that's happy to pick up your trade. Go for it; impart all that you've learned over the years.

Day 49: Seven Things Grandpa Taught Me Our Kids Should Know, II

Grow The Potential of Rich Soil: If you've learned anything about me, you know I love gardening and harvest. I remember the first time my mother and grandfather had all my brothers, sister and I come out to the back yard to work in our new garden-to-be. It was the very first time and it was cultural shock for city kids.

Grandpa had gotten the field disked and the rows formed. That day we planted, corn, peas, water melons, tomatoes, okra, butter beans, cucumbers, sweet potatoes, I could go on forever. We actually put the seeds in and I went back the next day to check on them.

You see the reason I can remember, is because after we planted them we had to chop them, after that then harvest them. Chopping them means; to keep the grass and weeds out from around them. The grass and weeds will choke the plant and smother it to death stopping the plants from producing.

Sounds like Jesus' story of the Seed and Sower, right. (Smile) The Arkansas soil is like nothing I've ever seen before. Mostly, everything produced bountifully every year. We would take it to market. I remember the cold mornings; you had to get out there before it got hot. For if you didn't, you would be considered lazy.

It grew so bountiful; the other reason, you had to hit it was, the fruit of the plants would grow too large and would be no good for market. There were plants that had a bite to it, like okra, peaches, cucumbers, they all would make your hands raw and itch you to death, well almost, at least I thought so.

When we birth our ministry there, we will have very large community gardens. Since I have been here in Texas my garden skills have turned to its cousin landscaping.

I've won yard of the month several times in my neighborhood, in the past. I planted thousands of tulips for my wife and my senior pastors for years. I did every spring with plenty pictures. I love the dirt!

3. Teach Discipline, Respect And Courage: Grandpa, Guns And Hunting

I'm really sad to see that a lot of my brothers and sisters in Christ feel they have to show their guns off, in this time and season. We are in a season that the hearts of men are being revealed. As an avid hunter, I grew up with many guns, and still so.

We were taught respect for guns very well by our Grandfather. We learned how to handle a gun and especially the dos and don'ts in gun handling. We were taught to NEVER EVER point a gun at another person. You never play around with guns or be careless around guns.

My brothers and I always had our guns sitting in the corner behind the door to the outside of the house. Just to think about it, one of the reasons why they were there, dinner might run across the yard at any moment (smile).

Here's a true story. I was raised by a single mother, a lot of you know that. Thanksgiving was coming and my mother was running short on funds. She was single with six teenagers. We were wondering what we would do for Thanksgiving dinner the next day. Well that evening three ducks decided to land in our pond that's behind our house. Can you believe it? My brother got all three of them.

We had duck instead of turkey, we were all very thankful. If you know duck hunting, you know there's no sneaking up on ducks. So, that was our miracle provision for that day. I still love hunting to this day; my favorite is deer hunting. Because all my life hunting rabbit, raccoon, squirrel, I never saw a deer. You wanna know why? The generation before me killed them all. But since then, they have changed the law, they are coming back strong.

Here's a funny story my wife tells about me. We were in our first few years of marriage and still getting to know each other. To make a long story short, right before my birthday, she figured she would ask my Creator what would really, really bless me. She wanted to surprise me with something she couldn't possibly know about me, yet.

We chose not to live together before marriage, so we had quite a bit of learning in marriage. Anyway, she says God told her to buy me a gun, a hunting gun. To say the least, she was surprised but went shopping for a gun. According to her, it was too confusing in knowing what to get. So, she told me the whole story...I ended up going with her to pick out my first .30-06, hunting rifle, called by most the deer gun.

Through hunting it was developed in my life respect, patience, discipline, courage, accuracy, long suffering, self-control and many more I could add to this list. I could talk about hunting forever, so I'll stop right here.

Day 50: Seven Things Grandpa Taught Me Our Kids Should Know, III

Lay The Foundation For Becoming A Fisher Of Men: It's great to reminisce about fishing with Grandpa. I love fishing but not as much as I like hunting. I have about a hundred fishing stories, so I won't wear you out; I'll only tell you one.

My grandpa was an excellent fisherman and huntsmen. As a shooter, I saw him shoot a bird out of the sky with one shot with a 22 pistol at about 70 feet away. My eyes were bucked and it was on for me being a hunter from that day on.

Fishing was of another sort, I loved it. I remember the weekends the men would come from everywhere to fish together. My chore was to get up and dig the worms for the fishing trip for me and with my brothers. It was good eating; we would catch coolers of fish especially Croppies, Brim (Perch), Catfish, Buffalo fish.

Sometimes, we would cook them on the lake in a big cooking pot. Umm delicious! One of my favorite lakes was Bear Creek Lake in Arkansas, beautiful. You can Google it. My wife and I still go there. As a child with Grandpa, we would fish until noon and then swim until the evening. When we got out of the water we would be little ash balls.

I would always pretend I was Jacques Cousteau while swimming in the deep water, maybe only fifteen feet. It was some of the best times in my life. As a fisherman, I learned the great skills of being an Angular and the beginning of being a good cook. My grandfather would make Fish Head Soup. If I had his recipe I would have a restaurant. I would only sell that soup and make a million dollars.

I think I bout got it! The recipe that is. Here are some of the lakes that I went to as a young fella: Cowbow, Bear creek, St. Francis, Spread Lake, White Hall Lake, Lange River, Long Lake Dream River; (I was baptized there) and many more. I can't wait to take my grandkids to many of them, like my grandfather did me and my brothers.

I can say fishing growing up set the foundation for becoming a fisher of men for the Gospel. I love fishing in the natural and I love being a fisher of men for Christ. Either way, it circles back around to Grandpa and his passion for fishing. I love him for taking the time to impart the things he did into his grand kids.

5. Pass An Appetite For Life: Chef and Cooking

I talked about Grandpa's Fish Head Soup earlier. In general, he was an awesome cook. I learned we were eating on the low end of the hog, when we had that soup. You know it's what po folks could afford to make. Well, maybe in thought. In that day nothing was thrown away, so they used the fish head to make a soup.

It's like use what you have leftover. Grandpa had a hog farm along with chickens, goose, hunting dogs, and a horse named Smitty. We would try to run him down to ride. You can imagine how that worked out.

Each year we would slaughter a hog and the community would show up; I loved this season. He had a smokehouse and he would smoke some of the meat and sometimes put the fish heads to dry out in the smokehouse. Grandpa would make this tomato based soup, fish soup that was delicious.

In the smokehouse he would have slabs of smoked bacon. We would cut a chunk in the morning and slice it for breakfast. It was pretty awesome with grits. I remember him cooking a large pot of grits in the morning and saying, "Have some." Of course, I would!

He would cook a large cast iron skillet of cornbread for him and me. I'm pretty sure my brothers would devour it, though I can't remember them there at this moment. He loved his with butter milk. I tried it, but to me, it was a much acquired taste. I noticed one generation had a certain combination of food they loved and swear by it. But the next generation would pretty much abhor it. Buttermilk and cornbread was one of those things for me.

So, the seed of my love for cooking and eating came from those special moments with Grandpa. With my cooking skills, I would get jobs at the famous Camel Lot Hotel in Little Rock Arkansas. In its hay-day my life shifted when I worked for them in food and socializing with people. I would go on to cook at Denny's and K-Bobs; both restaurants established me for life in the food industry.

The word of God says that your gift will make your way in Gods Kingdom. I have cooked on several occasions for our pastors in past years at their functions. I was honored to do it. Oh yes, I am the cook of the house. Earma says she loves it! Check out some of my food pictures on my Facebook page. My dream is to open a Catfish restaurant that only sells Catfish and fresh Fries.

I encourage you to explore cooking with your children. If they're interested pass those family recipes on to the next generation. They might not all end up interested in cooking but keep looking. It may show up in your grandkids, like me and my Grandpa. Share your passion for life and cooking with your children and your children's children...

Day 51: Seven Things Grandpa Taught Me Our Kids Should Know, IV

Give Good Character, Work Ethics and Wisdom: Now, you know I had to talk about hard work. I heard the stories of my grandfather's great strength. Stories, like him picking up the end of a car and moving it. Or before that in the horse and buggy days, he hit a horse on the butt and brought him to his knees. Why did he do that? I heard because the horse had gotten stubborn and wouldn't go any further. They were on their way to church and the horse needed to take them.

I wrote many of my Grandpa stories in my book, *Healing the Wound of A Fatherless Generation.* It can be shipped to you in a few days from Amazon.com

Our chores were always before us on a farm. My mother lived on a one-acre lot. My grandfather had more acreage and the grass grew always like a jungle. We all lived on an eighty-acre farm. In our back yard, if you missed a week of cutting the grass, it would be two feet tall.

We would have to use a swing blade to lower it first, before using a lawn mower to cut it. That was the mild work. We chopped the garden once a week, fed the hogs, help with work around the barn, the list could go on. As a warning, I think chicken poop is the worst smelling thing on earth. If you bring it in the house on your feet, you'll know it.

I remember we chopped cotton for six dollars a day, eight hours a day in full sun. I got my work ethic from growing up on a farm and being a country boy. Hard work builds good character. Now when I say this, in my heart I'm not bragging but I feel it's true. I've not met many that could out work me.

That hard work ethic has brought many promotions to me, in the natural on my jobs and in the kingdom of God. So, don't be afraid to teach your children hard work. They will grow up and be much better people because of it.

The word of God says God worked six days and rested on the seventh. With that in mind, yes we can enter into the Sabbath rest of God in our day but keep hard work a part of your life and your children's lives.

7. Love The Word Of God And Set A Pattern: Bible Reading and Worship

Our house was right next door to Grandpa's house. When I was a little younger, right before we moved to Marianna, Arkansas from St Louis, we used to always get in trouble for throwing things in our neighbors' yard. So, when we got to Arkansas and building a house next door to Grandpa, we couldn't believe we could go to our Grandparents house anytime we wanted. We were like, (Are you sure Mom?) She would say, yes, and smile.

I have special memories of Grandpa sitting on the front porch and reading the word of God. (the Bible) It seemed like every morning he would be there in the cool beautiful Arkansas weather. I would often see him with tears running down his face. He was establishing something in me. I wouldn't know it for years. I'm pretty sure that he knew it!

My family and I are a family of music, between my brothers and I and sister. We played a dozen instruments. My brothers sang and played in gospel quartet groups. They would practice at our house and my Grandfather's house. The way they would say it in the old days. (Man, the Spirit would move.)

They would begin to stump back and forth and harmonize, sweat. The house would be shaking. Grandpa would always do the bass. He would go Boom, Boom, Boom, Boom and then the tears would flow. I got all that from him. I love to sing; I am a singing preacher.

I must admit my father was a singing preacher, too; he was good. I learned how to seek the Lord and worship from my grandfather. I must admit; I just figured that out. I thank him for it, because I am an ordained minister of the Lord and he helped qualify me. Love you Grandpa! Kudos to you and Grandma Beasley!

I could go on but I'll use self-control, and stop for now. I wanted to let you see part of my life through my eyes and my perspective. I have such a rich heritage to pass to this next generation. I suspect that you do, too.

I could've been crippled by bitterly divorced parents and the horrible event that changed our lives. But by the grace of God, I wasn't! The Lord graced and covered me. He used what the enemy meant for bad and turned it to good. He used it to make me stronger, wiser, and be a more compassionate person.

Instead of being mean and a vicious person, mad at the world because of my family's troubles, I'm a more compassionate person. And yes I cry a lot. But I'm not embarrassed, I can hold my own.

I think you should relook over your own life and see, how the Lord helped you to get over. You may see that more was given to you than you realize. With that in mind you have more to pass on than you first thought.

Stay thankful and appreciative and the Lord will reveal to you, the great things He has done in your life. And most of all, you have little faces looking toward you for what you have to pass to them and the next generation.

Day 52: Overcoming The Sins And Iniquities Of Our Forefathers, I

In my young life, I had a great friend. Now this friend didn't have a relationship with his father. I did know of his father. I met him, years before, I met my friend. This friend was just like his father. I knew it but he seemed to have no idea that he was. This is the reason why I'm writing this. I see the same story over and over again throughout my life with different people.

Back to my story, my friend's father was a partying man; he loved the clubs. If you needed drugs or alcohol, he was the person to go to and he was a woman's man; there was none other like him. This is a very hard saying but I feel it needful to warn a generation headed the wrong way. So, they don't suffer the same demise.

To do this, we of my generation have to take courage and expose the enemy, repent of the sins and iniquities that some of our father's generation fell prey to. And produce fruit in keeping with that repentance.

Well, this friend of mine is still living that life style. And he is still just like his father. I'm afraid for him that if he doesn't change, he will meet the same demise that his father did. I know and everybody knows, if he acts out his father's same circumstances, he will eventually pay the same price, where he reaped from the mountain of bad seeds he had sown and died a premature death.

The reason I titled with, *The Sins and Iniquities of Our Forefathers*, is because that's exactly what it was. And it shouldn't be passed from generation to generation. Now, don't get me wrong. I'm not lumping all fathers in this category.

There are lots of great fathers that are passing the blessing to the next generation. Some fathers are just weak and want to do better. But then there are others who have become or headed toward becoming just rebellious and disobedient.

I don't want that for you. I want you and me to overcome the sins and iniquities of our forefathers. We'll talk about how to do that a little later.

Alcohol

When I was growing up, God graced me to be able to see things in the generation of our fathers' and elders' life and learn from them. One of them was not to become an alcoholic like my father was and to do it at all cost. I saw certain lines I could not cross, if I wanted to not become an alcoholic.

The reason I say it that way is because I saw and experienced the price that was paid because of that sin and maybe even iniquity never broken. As you may know today, they don't call it a sin; they say it's a medical condition. If forced to call it that, I would describe it as a medical condition caused by sin.

Anyway, as a youngster I knew that I had to stay far from the abuse of Alcohol. I chose not to let that sin of iniquity take control of my life with the help of the Lord.

Smoking

I had another friend that smoked. At that time, I smoked cigarettes too, a pack a day for about eight years. My friend's father smoked too. He was a hard smoker. Because of being one, it eventually caused his death. Now, this is where the learning comes in.

You would think, if a person sees their father or mother leave this earth, way too soon, from an addiction, they would say to themselves, "Man, I have to stop that." Right? Wrong.

I hate to say it; that friend of mine is still smoking to this day. I suspect they haven't stopped since we started in junior high school. All of this equals to is, the flesh ruling a person's life without Christ and this shouldn't be.

Day 53: Overcoming The Sins And Iniquities Of Our Forefathers, II

In my young life, I have seen this spirit run wild, without restraint. I've seen the demise of families because of it. When I was a teenager before I was saved, I was in the club scene. I saw the older generation reap the consequences of unfaithfulness and the destruction of families it caused.

Once I got saved and filled with the Holy Ghost, I had to let that stuff (clubbing scene) go. But what really breaks my heart is I still see some of my old friends and family still doing that same old fleshy stuff. And I say to myself, where is the learning?

If we see our carnal fathers die because of living a life after the flesh. Shouldn't we see it and want to change. Or will we give in to the sin of iniquity and do the same as they did.

With God's help, far be it from me. We must have ourselves and the next generation in mind and make sure that the curse and iniquities of our forefathers are banished from our families.

Hindering God

One the main things that can hinder or prevent us from having the power in Christ to overcome the sins and iniquities of our forefathers is unforgiveness. As a son or daughter, we must learn to forgive. If you don't forgive it's like plaque in a vein, it will clog the blood flow and can eventually stop the heart.

We must forgive. It is as natural as the blood that flows throughout our body that give us life itself. If I hadn't forgiven my father for his mistakes I would have passed down unbelievable pain and trouble to the next generation.

Now, I know everything isn't perfect. You see we must jump leaps and bounds to see Christ come forth in our families. So, make sure you are doing one of the least of things and forgive. Because if you are not, you aren't receiving God's best for yourself.

Overcoming The Sins and Iniquities of Our Forefathers

I must say, I didn't see it coming, the enemy. The Lord has given me a sure foundation to stand upon and I'm thankful. But there is a sin of iniquity that is lurking around seeing who will answer his call. I say to you, don't pick up that phone! If you have seen your father battle a sin of any means. Don't answer the door when it comes knocking.

Allow that curse to be broken and begin a new chapter in your family's life. In Christ, we are new creatures. If it hasn't been broken in your family, start in your generation. You can make the fresh start! Start a new trend in living a life of righteousness.

I'm not saying it will be easy or you won't have to fight the fight of faith to see it change. But remember our weapons are not carnal but mighty in God to the pulling down of strongholds. You can do all things through Christ Jesus.

If we will allow Christ to reign and rule in our life, there is always victory in Jesus!

Day 54: A Conclusion Of Grace

I've come to a conclusion not long ago. In the scheme of things, when I think about growing up fatherless, I've summed up a few things. After all I've been through, I've come to the conclusion that the Lord has covered me better than I could've ever done for myself.

Now don't get me wrong, I've been through some tough times along with my family. But, the Lord has been good to me. I have to acknowledge that. You see the Lord must have known that I loved Arkansas all my life, especially when I was growing up as a city boy in St Louis, Missouri.

The grace the Lord gave to me and my family was, in itself: my mom, country living and my grandparents. To be truthful, I know this sounds a little weird, my life was so full, I didn't even miss my father that much. To me, it's even sad that I have to say that.

Yet, my grandparents were a redeeming factor that came into our life. My young life was full of hard work. We grew every plant that grows from seed: watermelons, peas, corn, okra, tomatoes, cucumbers, butter beans, sweet potatoes, Irish potatoes, purple hull peas, carrots, peanuts, and cantaloupe. I'll stop there because I could go on forever. Everything grew like the Jolly Green Giant.

We would plant it mostly from seed, and chop it to keep the weeds cut back until harvest, so that it would grow. We did every year and we sold some of it as produce. We ate like kings; sometimes we would cook a large pot of corn after we harvested it.

I would eat it until my lips were raw, by the way, that's what happens when you have brothers in competition with each other. And you talking about eating healthy, every year, was like a garden of paradise in central Arkansas.

My grandfather had hogs, chickens, several geese, and a horse that we had to chase down to ride, can you believe it? My brothers and I were hunters, we shot rabbits, squirrels, raccoons, quails, and ducks. I could cook every one of them to deliciousness.

We fished, almost, every weekend. I still love to fish. We caught bream, croppies, catfish, buffalo fish, bass and many other fish. Sometimes, we would cook them down on the lake.

Once a year, my Grandpa would harvest a hog; all the men in the community would show up and help in the process. It was right in the middle of hunting season. It was as heaven on earth to me.

Please forgive me but I must tell you all the details. I always knew when it was hog killing time, my Grandpa would put the pig in a certain place (barn room) so that he could clean him up before the slaughter.

The day of the slaughter, we would have this 55-gallon barrel of water boiling. Except for the gore, this season was most exciting for a young boy; it is the life of the country. After putting him down, we would remove all the insides of the animal.

We would have to do the grunt work as young boys, sometimes literally, me and my brothers. We would lower the hog in the hot boiling water and pull him out and scrape the hair off.

Then they would cut it up. I would see my grandfather give certain portions away to neighbors. The result of this harvest, we would eat high on the hog for at least a year at our house and my grandfather's, life was good.

I'm trying to not be too graphic to make you go run and screaming. I also noticed, it was something, how grateful they were in receiving it. I had no idea that some parts were a delicacy but I know now.

My grandfather had a smoke house, he would smoke some of the meat and salt some down. We had real bacon with the rind on it, about as thin as you could cut it, with grits every morning. I remember chitterlings being cleaned in the house.

I would go straight back out the door when they were cleaning them. My grandfather was the greatest cook. I picked up just where he left off. I love cooking and my wife swears by it, that it's that good!

I never went hungry, even though my mother raised us by herself, along with my grandfather and grandmother's help. In our community, all the neighbors pitched in; I lived in a community of about fifty or more homes, and we were a big family.

Here's some of their names, my mother Betty Ruth Brown, Mrs. Pearl, Mrs. Barbara, Mrs. Mattie Vaughn, Mrs. Holmes, My Aunt Suge, (Rev. Vivian Brown) spiritual mother, Mrs. Bernice, Mrs. Rachel Lee, Mrs. Mayrene Brown, another spiritual mother for me.

Mrs. Alma Jones, Mr. and Mrs. Berry, Mrs. Ruth Gaines, Mrs. Pearl Jones. All of these families made sure that I stayed in line, most of the time when you entered their house, it was customary to hear them say to you if you were hungry and they were eating was, "Have some?"

Meaning do you want something to eat. Of course, being a youngster that loved eating, I would be there with a big smile saying, yes ma'am! They probably all said, we want to give them something to eat because, Betty has all those boys.

I love them all. They are part of the reason that I'm writing this story and I am who I am. They gave me a little of heaven when I was growing up in that part of my life. I am persuaded that their rewards will be great in heaven. I love them for it.

So I have come to this conclusion...

The Lord has been good to me. Despite all that I and my family went through, troubles from a broken family and our parents broken marriage. The Lord has been so good to me, I could not write all that he has done for me, there would not be enough pages to record it, and his goodness toward me. It would take a thousand books and a life time to write it.

So, all I can say for now is, "I thank you Lord!" You have been good to me. After my book that I wrote on this matter, "Healing the Wounds of a Fatherless Generation," blogs, the devotional, confessions, tears, rejections, misunderstanding, pains, and forgiveness, I have concluded that your love covers a multitude of sin. I thank you Lord for your grace that covers us so well.

Day 55: Why Have A Spiritual Father?

One of the very important reason why you should have a father, (spiritual father). Here's a story: When I was a kid in St. Louis Mo, I think I was about 5 or 6 years old. For some reason my brothers and I where deciding to act a little bad that day. I think we were walking home from school.

We decided to climb up on this commercial building just for the fun of it. I was to young so I had to stay on the ground that day. The next thing I knew my two older brothers where dancing on top the building having fun. All I could do was look and wish. At that very moment guest who passed by? Dad, and we saw him and we all said, oh boy!

As in, we are in trouble, and we were. I remember the interrogation. Dad said, did I see you guys on top of a building dancing. My two older brothers said, No, No that wasn't us and they were very adamant about it.

Then the question came to me and I couldn't help myself, and I said. We did it, yes we all did it. My brothers got a whipping but I didn't. My big brother was making fun of me a while ago about that story and said, yes that was the preacher in him, even then.

I told you that story because that was the effect of the "Father principle." that I am talking about. You see if you have a father or a spiritual father presence in your life there will be no foolishness in your life to speak of.

The reason why there won't be, because there will always be repercussions, and who want that! Make sure that you are covered, and be fathered.

Day 56: Joab's Insecurity

Now, for that example from the Word of God, I promised earlier. I wrote a book *In The Spirit Of Leadership* and it has a chapter in it about a character in the Bible by the name of Joab. This man and his brothers were spiritual sons of King David. Joab was, also, a great general for King David. There was a situation where a man was trying to defame King David and it was General Joab's job to rid the kingdom of him.

This man ran into a city and Joab followed him there. Joab and his men began to tear down the city wall. A wise lady came out and said to Joab, "Why are you tearing down our wall?" He said to her, "Because you have my master's enemy within. And we will tear your city's wall down until we get to him."

She said to him, "We are called the peaceful of Israel. And said, I will talk to my people and deliver him to you."

Moments later, they threw his head over the wall to Joab and his men. They promptly left the city.

Now you see Joab was rowdy, and he didn't take no mess from his enemies. But it was recorded, he was so insecure he would lose his very life because of it. He killed three men, Amasa, Abner, and even David's son Absalom when David told him not to, because of his insecurities.

They all were considered better men than he, and he was afraid they would surpass him. He was a great man but he was so insecure that he would never listen to his authority. He only did what he thought would lead him to a self-promotion. He would mow over people like they were grass. Oh yes, that is a huge clue with insecurities.

Insecurity is from the enemy. Lucifer was insecure. He said to himself, "I will ascend higher than the throne of God."

And he knew, good and well, he couldn't or shouldn't. From the definition I wrote of insecure, do you see any of them ruling in your life? If you do, it's real important that you receive healing. Because without it (healing), that wound can cause you to lose many battles in the Lord. It can even lead to bitterness and eventually a bitter root that grows up to defile many.

Ultimately, Jesus is our security. In Him we can find our true self. Christ has given us our identity that resides within Him. As we read and do his word and his will, we become more and more like Him. And the less, we will be satisfied with staying insecure.

When we know who we are in Him, we won't be showing our self-off. The more we're like him, the less we operate through insecurities, mean and grumpy to everyone we meet.

Here's a test for yourself; it's simple. So, don't get nervous.

Hang out with a secure person for a while. It will be better if they are a leader over you, then you can follow. Look at yourself and do some comparing. See if and where you may need to change. This is very important. Because if we're not careful, we can end up running everybody off, with a string of broken relationships everywhere. Then you're left all alone, full of insecurities, mean and bitter. I don't want this for you.

So I charge you to make this an assignment for yourself. If there are any of those words on that list residing within you. Put yourself to work and work them out and let the Lord completely heal you, and make you secure in Him. There's security in Jesus.

Day 57: Impress Them On Your Children

These commandments that I give to you today are to be on your hearts. Impress them on your children. Talk about them when you sit at home and when you walk alone the road, when you lie down and when you get up. Tie them as symbols on your hands and bind them on your forehead.

Write them on the doorframe of your houses and on your gates. As a son I was raised with the word of God set before me. As a father we raised our sons with the word of God ever before them.

Our sons as loving fathers are raising their children with the word set before them. If you want to have a successful family life, you will set the word of God ever before your family and children and you will have good success! Deuteronomy 6:6-9

ABOUT THE AUTHOR

Varn Brown is a five book Christian Author and Pastor including *The Character of King David, In the Spirit of Leadership, Healing the Wounds of a Fatherless Generation* and Co-Author of *A Devotion to Serve*. Also, he is an ordained second generation Baptist minister. He served as an Armorbearer and a Helps Ministry Leader for twenty years at Covenant Church, Carrollton Texas. He is co-founder of Grace Covenant Church, Nasa Ministries, and Armorbearers International. Varn lives in Dallas, Texas with his wife Earma. They have two adult children Varn, Jr., Khrystopher and five grandchildren Adrianna, Myleigha, Imani, Vaylen and Micah, Jr.

Other Books And Resources

- Healing The Wounds Of A Fatherless Generation (original book)
- In The Spirit Of Leadership
- The Character Of King David
- In The Spirit of Armorbearing Devotional: A Devotion To Serve

Visit Varn at http://varnbrown.com for other books and resources.

Notes

Confession and acknowledgement is good for the soul. — Varn Brown

Notes

Now no chastisement for the presents seemeth to be joyous, but grievous: nevertheless, afterward it yieldeth the peaceable fruit of righteousness unto them which are exercised thereby. — Hebrews: 12:11

www.ingramcontent.com/pod-product-compliance
Lightning Source LLC
LaVergne TN
LVHW011913080426
835508LV00007BA/512